COVENANT OF
BROTHERS

COVENANT OF BROTHERS

how to build relationships that unlock increase

Bishop Rich Conte
& Dr. Al Purvis

CIP information
Covenant of Brothers
Publisher: Purvis, Alan
ISBN 978-0-9782667-4-5
Printed and distributed by:
Continuum Media division,
World Mission Continuum
Box 32056
Edmonton, AB
Canada T6K4C2

Covenant of Brothers

Printed in Thailand

2014, Continuum Press

Charge to the Reader:

I challenge you to increase your leadership influence exponentially by investing in others as though you were investing in yourself.

Al Purvis

COVENANT OF BROTHERS

CONTENTS

COVENANT OF
BROTHERS

INTRODUCTION

Covenant bond: a game changer.

Covenant of Brothers is less about the win-win benefits of networking or the synergy of unified effort and more about the release of supernatural Kingdom power through a covenant between brothers. Rich Conte, an American missionary to the Philippines and Al Purvis, a Canadian missionary based in Thailand met at a conference in Singapore. Over the next two years their ministries grew together and exploded into a powerful Great Commission force across the Asian frontier.

This is not a covenant for covenant's sake but as David and Jonathan saw the future of Israel, these two missionaries cut covenant around a vision that is taking the world by storm. In this story you will discover some precious and well-kept secrets of how to succeed in the supernatural Kingdom.

COVENANT OF
BROTHERS

Chapter 1

A COVENANT DAWNS

You can't make this stuff up.

Rich Conte

In 1983, I landed in the Philippines as a young missionary from America. For the first 10 or 15 years I struggled along, seeing God do some things; some people getting saved, some getting healed, but seeing nothing really dramatic as far as growth goes - nothing really amazing. So we launched our own church planting organization and called it Rivers of Life. By the grace of God, in the next six years, we planted five churches. They were typically small, sort of independent churches that survived and grew as best they could.

This was my first twenty years of ministry accomplishment; I got married, had three children, and planted a handful of churches. Since I was the top guy, nobody was speaking into my life, nobody encouraging me, nobody to turn to when I had struggles. I was pretty much burned out, not backslidden, just worn out. I was still going through the motions, but did not have much fire or vision in my life.

My wife, Ning, and I received an invitation in the mail to a 'Times of Refreshing' conference for missionaries to be held in

Singapore. We decided to go just because we needed the refreshing, and it was free, and that's where we met Al and Terry. Well, at first we just met them casually. All I found out was that he was a missionary in Thailand and had been there about as long as I had been in the Philippines.

I was sitting in one of the conference sessions listening to some guy from Texas, I don't remember his name. He was calling people out of the audience of maybe two hundred missionaries. He would have them stand up and then prophesy over them. I was sitting in the back and I was desperate, "God, I need a word! God, I need a word! God, please give me a word!"

The session ended. I didn't get a word and I was disappointed, a bit discouraged. The spiritual part of the conference seemed to be over and we were all being ushered down to the hotel swimming pool for a group photo. As we were moving toward the pool area, the guy who had been ministering caught up to me and put his arm around me and said, "I had a word from the Lord for you during the session but we ran out of time." And he began to prophesy over me. So I'm almost in tears at this point. Then I noticed Pastor Al standing about twenty-five feet away. I didn't really know him but the Holy Spirit said, "Go and ask that man to pray over you."

You've got to imagine this picture: I'm burnt out, I'm weary, I'm asking the Lord for a word, and feeling disappointed. The next thing I know the preacher from Texas is prophesying over me a very accurate word. As soon as he walked off the Holy Spirit said to me, "Go get that man to pray for you!" So I walked over to Pastor Al and I said, "Would you mind, could you just pray for me?" So Al started prophesying over me and I went down under the Spirit, under the power of God. Just bang right there, poolside in this fancy hotel. And I don't go down. I'm not the guy that just goes down every time I get prayed for. I mean Rodney Howard Brown prayed for me and I didn't go down. I ain't going down if it ain't God! I'm a little tenacious that way. But as Al was prophesying over me, the power of God hit me and I went down. My wife was with me, people were gathering and I couldn't get up.

Al Purvis

When Terry and I boarded the plane for Singapore, we were probably about as tired and burned out as all the other missionaries we were about to meet. Bill and Emogene Kaiser had done a bunch of these 'Times of Refreshing' conferences in Europe and decided they wanted to bless the missionaries in Asia as well.

We had been in Thailand for 17 years and the stress of fighting alone for that long had worn us down. There were many missionaries in Thailand, so it's not like we were breaking open a new country, but God had sent us to pioneer some certain areas that were difficult; so in the vision God had given us, we were alone. Canadians are pioneers and it's a strength God often uses us for in spiritual advancement in hard places.

We began the ministry in Thailand in 1981 by gathering 27 orphans, most of them from among the refugees streaming into Thailand after the Vietnam War. That became our life: a small rented house in congested Bangkok, packed with our own three kids plus the 27 and never a day off.

Terry and I knew what cabin fever was; we were living in a little snow-bound cabin in the bush of northern Alberta when we packed up our kids and their teddy bears and moved to Thailand. Once in Thailand, we found ourselves stuck in a house until we learned enough of the language to get around. We began to travel by offering our help to other ministries. By that time there were 36 of us. We would pack a bag for each of us, drums, guitars and amps and stuff the whole thing into a 1980 Mazda pickup. We would travel a thousand kilometers on horrendous roads to help set up and invite people to open air evangelistic crusades. Our kids were the first worship band ever to travel and minister around Thailand.

The apostolic call was in our hearts and we could see hints of it working through our ministry but we knew little about it. Once our kids began reaching adulthood, we wanted to shift into church planting and decided to spend a few years in Canada to prepare and learn. This was the early '90's, the Victory Church in Lethbridge, Alberta, was led by Dick & Joan Dewert and this became our obvious destination. Victory was the fastest growing church planting movement in Canada and that's where we had connections. We plugged into Victory's apostolic vision and renewed our relationships with George and Hazel Hill and the growing number of leaders they were mobilizing into church planting across Canada. After four years of working with Victory in Canada, we returned to Thailand and began the exciting work of planting our first church, but we ran into a lot of exhausting, energy-expending problems.

So we flew to Singapore that day, really looking forward to a 'Time of Refreshing.' I remember making up my mind that when we got to the conference I would find other missionaries to encourage and see if that wouldn't encourage me as well; it usually does. We noticed Rich and Ning leaving the breakfast buffet and looking for a seat. I motioned them to join us at our table. We talked about generalities, our lives as missionaries and the work we were involved in. I could see that Rich was a church planter, an apostle, but he looked puzzled when I talked about apostolic ministry. He had planted a bunch of churches but it didn't seem that they were working together in apostolic relationship. I thought, "God has put something amazing in this guy but he doesn't see it. Maybe I will get a chance to lay hands on him and declare the Word of the Lord for a shift into apostolic ministry." That's what came up out of my spirit.

The conference ended with a group photo by the pool. We were on our way to pack our things when Rich and Ning came up and asked us to pray for them. We prayed and I began to prophesy and Rich went down under the power of God. I try not to let that happen when I am delivering a word from God, but Rich got away on me. This was an intense touch of the Holy Spirit, God was doing something deep and we didn't really understand the ramifications. The hotel staff asked if they could call a doctor but I assured them he would be okay. Eventually we helped Rich up, and he and Ning headed for their room. Rich had given me his email address earlier so I would just email him and try to keep in touch.

Chapter 2

COVENANT FORWARD

The move toward enlargement.

Rich Conte

And so, when I finally got up I was drunk in the Spirit. I couldn't walk and I am not one of those guys that do this kind of thing. I'm pretty much the opposite, I'm pretty conservative. This experience marked me. I'd just been prophesied over and my wife had to help me back to the room - that's how I met Pastor Al. So after that I figured there's got to be something here, you know? I thought back on little things we'd shared during the conference, about what he's doing, his organization. Then we began to email back and forth and we just began to build a kind of friendship. When he came to the Philippines, he was coming for another meeting. I immediately invited him to come and minister to our churches. He would also invite me to Thailand a couple of times.

Over a period of two or three years we were just going back and forth. He'd come and minister to our churches and I'd go over to Thailand. And of course the whole time he's sharing with me the Victory vision, his vision, the vision that he has for all of Asia. And he's trying to sell me on the vision. Well, at that time I was independent.

Another word for independent is 'alone.' I thought we were doing okay and I guess that we were doing okay, and that's about all. But as Ning and I started to pray about it I'd say to her, "This relationship is really good."

Another thing I like to say is that Pastor Al is the first missionary I met that I really liked. And the reason I say that is because he did in Thailand what I did in the Philippines; he became Thai. He learned the language, dressed like the people, ate what they ate, treated the people as if they mattered to him. He treated them as equals, and not many missionaries know how to do that. That's what I really liked about him; he was just down to earth, not trying to prove anything to anybody, but just being faithful.

And then of course he had this vision for all of Asia, which was in my heart as well. And I had to admit that where I was in the Philippines, although we were doing a good work, it was going slow. Even though I had a big vision, it would be impossible to fulfill from where I was at that point. So over time Al and I developed our relationship, and God began to speak to our hearts. Ning and I began to see the tremendous potential, the wonderful advantages of having a mentor, of being in close covenant relationships. Thailand is a more strategic location for reaching Cambodia, Vietnam, Burma and Laos. You can get to all of these places by land from Thailand. In the Philippines we're in the middle of the ocean.

So we began to see the potential of being connected, and we began to pray that way. As I said, at that time we had five churches, all independent. As my wife and I prayed, we became more convinced that this was God's leading. So I gathered all of our Filipino pastors and said, "Look guys, we really feel like God is leading us to come under this ministry, but I'm not forcing you to make this decision. This is what my wife and I feel that the Lord is leading us to do. If you choose not to join us it's okay, we're not having a split, we're not having a division or an argument. We can go our separate ways and still continue as friends." And by the grace of God, they all decided to join the Victory vision.

We started by joining our five churches together under the banner of Victory Churches of Asia. At that point I had been in the ministry for almost 20 years. I had planted three other churches under another organization, making a total of eight churches planted in 20 years. We joined the vision in 2001 and as part of Victory Churches of Asia we've grown to 26 churches in only eight years. So 20 years plugging along and then "suddenly." You can really see how the anointing comes down through covenant relationships. Have you heard the saying, "The anointing is caught, not taught"? The anointing passes through covenant relationships and there is literally an exponential growth that begins to take place. The Bible says, "One can put a thousand to flight, two can put ten thousand to flight."[a] Not two thousand, but ten thousand. There's an exponential thing that happens.

After joining Victory Churches under Pastor Al, we met with Dr. George Hill and connected with the world-wide vision. Victory leaders began to impart into our lives, began to teach us to think big, dream big, believe big. And we caught the idea of moving from our small city into Manila to plant a church. So we formed our Philippines team into prayer groups and began to pray for some months. The Lord used Dr. George to challenge us to plant a church with 200 people attending the first Sunday. I had never heard of such a thing in all of my life, but it got down on the inside of me and I began sharing that with our team and assuring them, "We are going to plant a church with

200 on the first Sunday." I shared that with them for about a month. Everyone was behind it enthusiastically and then I felt the Holy Spirit say, "I want you to double it."

I thought, "God, I've never even pastored a church of 200, now you're expecting me to plant a church not of 200, but 400 on the first Sunday?" But I knew it was from the Lord, so we just began to declare that and say, "We're going to plant a church of 400 on the first Sunday." After five months of serious prayer walks through various neighborhoods in the area we had grown a small group of 20 core people. Pastor Al brought a team of missionaries from Thailand to help advertise and prepare the launch. And by the grace of God, on September 21, 2003 we opened our first Sunday service in Manila.

We exploded from a group of 20 to 450 adults in the opening service, 300 of them came to the altar weeping. So that's how we started. That's God! That's just God! From there we have grown to about 2,000 people in ten years and have grown to 28 churches, several of them are quite large. That's the power of covenant relationships. That's the power of the anointing that is imparted not just caught - it's transferred because you are ready for it, you've paid a price for it - like in the story of Elijah and Elisha. Elisha got a double portion because they were so connected. It's been great.

Now for me, like I said, being independent is another way to describe being alone. I'm not alone anymore. I've got somebody I can turn to, somebody I can run to, somebody I can bounce stuff off of. There's synergy, a cross-pollination going on all the time that is now working across ten countries in Asia. We're sending our people to Thailand and other places and they're sending people to the Philippines. Everybody benefits, the ministry grows, and we just get along so well.

We are good friends even though Al is pretty much my boss. We're just good friends and it's close to the best decision I ever made in my life.

I always say there were three important decisions that I made in my life. First of course, was receiving Christ. Second was marrying my wife, I made a good choice there, and the third was joining Victory Churches with Pastor Al. That was the third best decision I made in my life, it's just been really good.

Al Purvis

Developing the relationship between Thailand and the Philippines was costly, for both Rich and myself. But the other option was to just keep doing things the same old way and forget about approaching the next level of vision.

There were travel costs back and forth over our little stretch of the Pacific. But the real cost, the one we tended to question, was that we were approaching each other to lay down our ministries for the benefit of the other. Both of us would risk investing our reputations and ministry accomplishments into a relationship where 'mine' is no longer 'mine' but 'ours.' The real question is, "Why would anybody do that?" Why would Jonathan give up his right to the throne of Israel for David? Men make deals for what they can gain, but covenants are made for what we can give. And the biggest things we give are our independence and our individual identity.

I know that what God has given me is for Rich too, for Peter in Pakistan, and Joel and Harley in Cambodia, and Joseph in India, Ezekiel in Malaysia, Prem in Nepal, Chaminda in Sri Lanka and for anyone who is willing to connect with us through covenant.

If I believe God has given me ownership in a vision then I had better gather and empower the people of that vision. It's not my vision; I got it from George Hill, Dick Dewert and other leaders who were willing to walk in covenant with me when I needed them. These men saw some potential in me that they believed was worth investing into. Vision allows us to see potential, and covenant is how we invest in that potential. Great men and women will invest in you if they see you are a person of commitment.

(endnotes)

a Deuteronomy 32:30

Chapter 3

COVENANT IMPLICATIONS

What does this look like?

Al Purvis

When Terry and I got home from our honeymoon, we slipped right back into helping around the church. One evening I was standing at the door of the church waiting to take Terry home but she couldn't leave because the pastor had given her another task. She was used to being single and free to work at the church whenever needed, and now it looked like I was going to be left standing there alone because of the relationship between our pastor and my new wife. I jumped in, "We're married now and we need to go home." This was an adjustment between two covenants.

If you think about it, you have covenant relationships with a lot of people and sometimes the covenants overlap, and even conflict. Jonathan had a father-son covenant with King Saul and a covenant of brothers with David. Those two covenants clashed violently because Saul was self-centered and greedy. That covenant put Jonathan in a difficult place; he gave David the crown of Israel but ended up dying on Mount Gilgal with Saul.

Both Rich and I have other covenants that we walk in; we have other friends and other ministries we relate to. Covenants based on love don't clash, but covenants used for control will clash, sometimes violently. I don't think I have ever ordered or pressured Rich to do anything for me (except to write this book), because both of us are always looking for ways we can bless and promote each other, and others. The relationship is not master-slave, boss-employee, or leader-follower. We are equals through covenant, because we are both leaders in the same vision. Neither of us have ever raised our voices, clenched our teeth, turned red in the face, or rolled our eyes at the other. Some people think it's because we have become Asian on the inside, but really it's because we're looking through the eyes of a covenant based on love. So even in the midst of extreme difficulties, we don't see conflict but challenges that we are committed to defeat together.

Covenant is a relationship that seeks to always do the best thing for the other person, like you would for a son or a brother. In Victory Asia we work together through relationship, not coercion or control. We fight for this as a core value of our ministry culture.

Some leaders are in conflict continually: disapproving, confrontational, hurtful. It's either because they are immature or they aren't really in covenant or both. Covenant is not a means to gain leverage for what I want from you but a commitment to empower you. If I am empowering you I will not be in conflict with you. If a marriage covenant is in conflict we say it is unhealthy, and it happens because of some wrong expectations in the relationship.

When we are in true, healthy covenants, we can have a marriage covenant, team covenants, business covenants, a church membership covenant, and they can all get along together. In a world of perfect hearts, covenants don't clash. We don't have to break one covenant to enter another; the nature of a covenant is that it can't be broken. Divorce of any covenant is very painful because it is contrary to love and honour.

I am in many covenant relationships, each one playing a certain role in my life. These covenants are powerful because they represent someone's love for me and their commitment to my good. They are powerless for the purpose of making demands on each other. If a leader becomes exclusive or jealous over you, like Saul was jealous of David's covenant with Jonathan, you know there's an unhealthy motivation. You may even be accused of breaking covenant, but unless you've been unfaithful, that accusation is just another Saulish attempt to manipulate you.

We understand both the purpose and commitment of each covenant relationship. The marriage covenant my wife and I walk in is more than just a commitment to get along as though we love each other; it is two people loving each other in person and purpose. Together we are changing the world! Our Thailand ministry team is absolutely the best and our covenant partners across Asia are amazing.

Pastor Eve Bassett and the Church of Abundant Life in Edmonton, Canada are our longest surviving leaders. We have been in covenant for well over 30 years and this covenant is about success in life and ministry. These are some of the folks who have always been there when we needed help and we are empowered by the amazing love and faithfulness they have shown Terry and I and the ministry in Asia. If you like my attitude toward blessing others, the credit for this one goes to our Pastor Eve. Through her tremendous example of keeping a right heart through every situation she has empowered us to aspire to do the same. In the same church Dr. Harland and Loretta Hendrickson founded this ministry, and this couple continues to be the single greatest champions of this vision.

Dr. Mervyn and Muriel Mediwake have been our closest spiritual parents during the past couple of decades. This covenant is one of personal life and heart issues. Papa Mervyn helps me sort through the crazy stuff we face in ministry on a personal level. Drs. George and Hazel Hill lead one of the best church planting movements in the world and having a personal relationship with them is a great honour. This covenant is the source of our inspiration for great exploits and plays a big role in the relationship Rich and I are reviewing in this book. Then there's all the covenant family who support us financially, send their kids to learn and work in this ministry, watch our television shows and pray for us.

Think of the many covenant relationships in your life, how they all fit together, and how they are very different from typical deals, contracts or networks - and much more powerful.

When Rich and I formed our covenant relationship, all of the covenants from my past met with an equally intricate set of covenants that make up his story. Rich and I did not have to break or annul any former covenant relationships, but this was a new step into the expanse of a greater level of vision. This new covenant satisfied a need that the others had not yet met. When we met Rich and Ning we were sensing an anointing on our ministry to expand across Asia. The idea wasn't to add the Philippines to some list of nations under our ministry but to work together to more effectively reach Asia with the gospel. Rich has helped me personally to stay on track. He's an example and pioneer of new church planting strategies and he's done a lot of things other nations can model.

Recently, Rich spent two weeks in Thailand teaching 'Church Planting' at our Victory Asia Bible College. We brought in our apostolic leaders from the other Asian countries to attend his classes. All of these leaders of nations are apostolic leaders in their own right and each one brings a particular gift of encouragement and empowerment into our company of apostles. This covenant thing is pretty amazing. It is the vehicle through which the dreams and visions of our hearts can be empowered.

We are brothers through covenant for the purpose of bringing God's Kingdom to Asia. This band of brothers includes apostolic leaders in Burma, Cambodia, China, India, Malaysia, Nepal, Pakistan, Vietnam, Sri Lanka, Rwanda, as well as Thailand and the Philippines; not to mention all the amazing pastors and leaders in the western world who support and encourage us so much it brings tears to my eyes. We are so very thankful for each one.

These are not lip service covenant relationships but high-end investments in each other - a lot of time is spent together and resources flow freely among us. What a glorious way to get the job done.

Chapter 4

UNDER COVENANT

I get the picture.

Al Purvis

A Roman centurion came to Jesus to ask for a miracle because his daughter was sick and near death. The soldier had figured out from the stories he'd heard that Jesus had authority over disease and demons because of some higher authority He was under - a name that worked in the supernatural realm just as the name of Rome worked in the political realm. He began his request by telling Jesus, "I too am a man under authority." He compared Jesus to himself because he saw Jesus as a centurion in the supernatural realm, just as he was a centurion in the natural realm. So if Jesus would give the command, nothing could stop the miracle. He told Jesus, "Just speak the word and my daughter will be healed."

In the mind of the centurion, Jesus had authority because He was under authority. We too must first be under God's authority in order for a covenant between brothers to be effective. The centurion knew the horizontal relationship worked because the vertical relationship was in place and Jesus responded, "I have not seen greater faith, even among the people of God." He said, "I can do nothing but what I see and hear from My Father." Likewise, we will not walk in the blessing of mutual covenant unless we first walk in covenant with God. This blessing is for, "Those who have made a covenant with me by sacrifice."

Flow From the Top Down

Rich and I are talking about how to powerfully fulfill your destiny in life and ministry from a position of mutual agreement. Agreement will direct and release power, but to connect with people who can empower us we must first be connected to God. In Him we see our future, tap into our inheritance, and find our place among the brothers of our destiny. No man can get there alone, but in order to walk with others we must genuinely walk with God.

The heroes of our faith are all men and women under covenant with God and I expect my significant destiny to unfold because, "I too am a man under authority and in covenant." I know God, and His power through covenant; therefore I can expect to walk in the empowerment of covenant relationships with my brothers.

The First Sacrifice

A man enters covenant with God and becomes a living sacrifice; otherwise he cannot expect to enter a covenant that requires sacrifice from others. There is no benefit to be gained by making a covenant for self-benefit; it just won't work. Such relationships are doomed to be broken through mutual disappointment rather than blessed through mutual sacrifice. Only a life in covenant with God is eligible for the power of a covenant between brothers. A life in covenant with God is a life lost to Christ, nevertheless Christ lives in me.[a]

David and Jonathan were men who walked humbly before God, so they cut one of the most powerful covenants known between men in the history of the world. Saul could not cut such a covenant or even understand it because of his pride and the manipulations that he held in his heart. His relationship with God was misplaced.

A covenant relationship with God has changed my heart and set me up for wonderful success. God said all the promises throughout the entire Bible are available to me through this covenant.

Vertical Beginnings

The success of my Christian life and ministry can be clearly traced back to when God spoke into my time of deepest frustration. As a new believer I was trying my best to serve God by preaching His message, but with nearly no results. Lack and confusion overruled my good intentions and I needed to know why. When I finally ended up on my face, God said, "Make a covenant with me." He explained covenant in one simple sentence, "I will do what I said I will do if you will act like what I said is true."

I agreed with Him and became a man under covenant.

From that day on I have paid attention to anything I could learn about covenant and found that 'covenant' is a well-kept secret. Most sermons and teachings I have heard about God's covenant were vague and some of the men who preached about them were critical of their leaders and dishonouring to God and other churches - they were not eligible themselves for a covenant of brothers.

Generally, people know that God is a covenant-keeping God,

yet they might not understand the requirements and benefits of His covenant. If we truly understand the covenant, we will be walking in the abundance of life He promised. I give an in-depth teaching about the power of our covenant relationship with God in my book 'On To Perfection.' 'Covenant of Brothers' is about the power of horizontal covenants, covenants between God's people.

The Horizontal Reveals the Vertical

John asked, "How can you say you love God whom you cannot see if you don't love the brothers you live with face to face?" Without a deep conviction of internal integrity we cannot succeed in covenant relationship with others. I can successfully love my wife in our marriage covenant because I know God's love. I can walk well with my spiritual fathers, brothers and sons because I walk well with God. We actually perceive and experience God's love by sacrificing for others as Jesus sacrificed for us. It's a spiritual law.[b] Covenant leaves no room for selfishness and the horizontal covenant can only be as successful as the vertical covenant.

When Rich and I first met, he was willing to be friends because of certain things he saw in our lives: We had been in Thailand a long time, we spoke Thai and we lived with Thai people. Rich could see that we held kindred convictions as missionaries. This is not some quirky criterion for friendship but you can see if a man loves God by how he loves people. If Terry and I had never joined ourselves to the people we came to minister to, I'm sure Rich and Ning would never have joined themselves to us. I could never expect to walk in covenant relationship with brothers without being a man under covenant.

I too am a man under authority and in covenant with God

through Jesus Christ and because that covenant is in place and healthy, it overshadows and empowers my covenant relationships with people. Covenant is the most powerful level of relationship in existence.

Covenant Quality

God is presently upholding all things by the "Word of His Power."[c] His Word has power because it is a covenant word, an unbreakable word. God says it like this, "If you can break My covenant with the day and My covenant with the night, so that there will not be day and night in their season, then My covenant may also be broken with David...."[d] He's giving a picture of just how absolutely certainly His covenant promises will come to pass. Just as His covenant guarantees His promises to us, a covenant between brothers becomes the guarantee of our trust in each other. An honourable man will swear to his own hurt and change not.[e] We become unstoppable when we can trust each other.

(endnotes)

a Galatians 2:20

b I John 3:16

c Hebrews 1:3

d Jeremiah 33:20

e Psalm 15:4

Chapter 5

FIVE COVENANT MEASURES

The value of a covenant relationship.

Al Purvis

In the 1800's Stanley was traveling through Africa looking for Livingstone. The continent was dark and dangerous and Stanley met impenetrable resistance - one of the most powerful chiefs in Africa stood against him as his enemy. Stanley's guide suggested he try making a blood covenant with the chief. As the story goes, the chief gave Stanley his spear in trade for Stanley's goat. This was a difficult choice for the foreigner who needed the goat's milk to sustain his health, but the other option was to return to England. Stanley and the chief mingled blood from their wrists and the covenant was cut. Stanley soon discovered that every tribe he met from that day on would bow to the spear he carried and give him anything he requested. With this spear he could have as many goats as he wanted and go wherever he wanted.

But this covenant wasn't about Stanley getting his way; it was about the greatest chief in Africa blessing the helpless foreigner by making him his brother. Why would someone do that?

The Greater Blesses the Lesser

A covenant is the forming of a relationship where the greater person blesses the lesser, and for the purpose of the covenant they become like brothers. Abraham became the friend of God through covenant. We find it amazing that the God who created all things cut a covenant with man and became our equal. This idea seriously offends the religious mind - the idea that man can have any position of equality with God. God is not intimidated by His creation and if He says I'm His son, a joint heir with Jesus, then it must be so.

Paul shows how the vertical covenant provides the picture and the power of the horizontal covenant. He defines our brotherly covenant as us, "...being like-minded, having the same love, being of one accord, of one mind. Let nothing be done through selfish ambition or conceit, but in lowliness of mind let each esteem others better than himself. Let each of you look out not only for his own interests, but also for the interests of others."[a] What a perfect picture of the covenant between brothers!

But Paul goes on to show that this only happens if we live in vertical covenant with God. We must, "Let this mind be in you which was also in Christ Jesus, who, being in the form of God, did not consider it robbery to be equal with God, but made Himself of no reputation, taking the form of a bondservant, and coming in the likeness of men. And being found in appearance as a man, He humbled Himself and became obedient to the point of death, even the death of the cross."[b]

When God as the greater, blesses me as the lesser, it does not diminish Him as though I was stealing His sovereignty. On the contrary, if I say no to His free gift of righteousness then I must remain as a worm in the dust, and the cross of Christ has won no victory for me.

He knows us. He knows that unless He changes us we will continue in depravity, but when He changes us through Christ's death and resurrection, we become His righteousness. God brought about this change by making a new covenant with Abraham and ratifying it through Jesus' blood. If we are Christ's then we are Abraham's seed.

God draws us into a covenant relationship with Himself to save us from sin and make us righteous before Him. Abraham believed God and it was counted to him for righteousness. What did he believe? He believed that Jesus would take all punishment for sin, condemnation of sin and the wages of sin. Abraham believed in the gospel of Jesus Christ.

Covenant is better than law. Law tells us how to obey but covenant empowers us from the inside out; now we can obey. Through this covenant, by the blood of Jesus, we are restored to our intended place of fellowship with Him.

More Than a Contract

Covenant is a much deeper relationship than a contract. A contract is an arrangement for providing one thing and receiving something of equal value from someone we otherwise might not trust. A contract works by ministering conditions and constraints but a covenant works by ministering love. A covenant changes the core motivation. Being in covenant with God we don't just act like Christians, we become Christians, Christ-like. Covenant, both with God and our brothers, does more than force certain behaviours, it changes our core values, it changes our heart. A covenant between brothers wants me to love you, sacrifice for you and empower you. Our covenant with God establishes my faith in His promises. I have the assurance that what I hope for will happen.[c]

Covenant Empowers Destiny

Covenant doesn't just hold us together, but empowers us mutually for our corporate destiny. In covenant we bless each other with all that we are and all that we have and we benefit from each other's strengths. Yet there's another fascinating aspect. When I give to you through our horizontal covenant relationship, God gives to me through our vertical covenant relationship. This tie between the vertical and horizontal covenants pushes us into the "...more than we can ask or think according to the covenant power that works in us,"[d] level of supernatural favour. In covenant we sacrifice for the good of the other so that God can bless us at a covenant level of favour, rather than a deserving level of favour. Keep this up and you will find that God begins to bless you in ways you didn't think about or ask for.

God's Love

God's covenant with us is a covenant of love: a legal right to His benefits, not because we deserve it but because His greatness chose to bless us, even in our smallness.

God doesn't expect us to understand this, but He does expect us to believe it. His best explanation is, "I set my love upon you because I love you,"[e] and He tells us in the New Testament that He "is rich in mercy, because of His great love with which He loved us."[f] How does that make sense? It will not compute in the mind but the heart clings to it and understands it.

The African chief chose to cut a covenant with Stanley because something touched his heart when he considered this lesser man and the impossible task he was trying to accomplish. That's how love works, no explanation needed. Stanley gave up his best possession at the chief's request. The covenant was not about a goat and a spear of equal value, it was about destiny. You have my permission to put this book down now, if there isn't something in you that yearns to help others reach their destiny. We were born for such exploits.

Covenant is the Way Forward

My destiny reaches fulfillment through covenants. In covenant we adopt fathers, brothers and sons. Remember, the greater blesses the lesser by fully sharing influence and resources. I follow my fathers, share with my brothers and give to my children, and it's all about fulfilling the destiny of my family, my tribe and my Kingdom.

In covenant we share our ideas, relationships and other resources as brothers, we trust each other as brothers, and we bless each other as brothers. But first we must be trusted by God.

(endnotes)

a Philippians 2:2-4

b Philippians 2:5-8

c Hebrews 10:22, 11:1

d Ephesians 3:20

e Deuteronomy 7:7-8

f Ephesians 2:4

Chapter 6

THE SPIRIT OF COVENANT

A different spirit.

Al Purvis

Know therefore that the LORD your God is God; he is the faithful God, keeping his covenant of love to a thousand generations of those who love him and keep his commands.[a]

An Opposite Spirit

One Easter Sunday, three men with rifles opened fire on the congregation of one of our Victory churches in Pakistan. One man was killed and several were hospitalized. The Pakistani news reported the killing as a dispute between Christians and Muslims over land ownership. When the news hit the papers in the west, a lady from a certain Christian denomination recognized the church building and contacted me wanting to know how this church had become a Victory church. The building had originally been built by their organization. I checked into it and discovered that the church had closed down and some of our team in Pakistan had revived it years later, under the name of Victory. Such conflicts can easily arise among Christian organizations anywhere in the world. I answered my new friend by promising that whatever we invest in Pakistan we intend to release fully to the local believers. I added that this issue is a perfect opportunity for her and I to act in the opposite spirit of the men who attacked our innocent brothers and sisters. She answered me in the same spirit of love. I was blessed! That kind of response does not exist outside of Christ's command to love one another - and that's the difference. In a few short years this church has tripled the size of its building and congregation and has gained great favour in the community.

Release

One of my spiritual fathers once told me, "When we stop releasing, we limit our potential." He was talking about the pre-determined willingness we all begin our Christian lives with - to give out, to treat others as we would have them treat us. The trouble is when we get old and battle-scarred from being taken advantage of or disappointed too many times, we can easily become afraid of the risk and begin to build security systems to protect what's ours. Then God becomes smaller in our lives. In the early days, our Victory vision was stated 'Reach, Teach, and Release' then it became 'Reach, Teach, and Mobilize'. Mobilize is more accurate to the apostolic ministry we do but we must keep 'Release' at the forefront of our attitudes and actions. That's the heart we began with.

It takes a great determination to be a blesser. Pastor Eve Bassett is probably my favourite blesser of all. She has survived more terrible circumstances than most people I know and yet has maintained a heart abundant in giving and blessing. She does crazy things, like the Sunday she recognized a pastor from another church sitting in the back row, received the Sunday offering, and gave the entire thing to him. The last time we were there she had the church put on a fundraising dinner in celebration of our 30 years of ministry in Asia. And over the course of the weekend dozens of people came up and prophesied blessing over Terry and I.

Sad to say, some of our missionaries come from churches that support them as minimally as possible and sometimes not at all. I can only imagine the reasons. Then there are the other churches that do everything they can to love on and support those they send; it's a totally different spirit. But the missionary as well with every other person must be careful not to be critical toward people who withhold or diminish us. Those are not covenant attributes so they hold no influence over us.

Withholders

Our heart and focus, especially as missionaries, is to be giving-minded rather than receiving-minded, because God is our source - and He is your source if you are a releaser. Our church on the mission field, made up of missionaries, national leaders, and students, gives more to missions than most western churches. Some years this amounts to over 50% of our gross income. This doesn't happen easily, we had to fight to gain this attitude and we fight to maintain it. Transforming our thinking from being receivers to givers is a major spiritual battle. You can't change from being a hoarder to a releaser without dealing with your fear of lack, no matter how much money you have or don't have. That shift from being the needier to the giver is something that Pastor Eve imparted to us once we were ready to hear it from God. We reached this level of generosity as a result of that covenant relationship. We honour her and follow her lead because we are certain she has our best in mind.

The withholder of blessing doesn't believe this, so covenant generosity doesn't come their way. The currency I'm talking about isn't money, it's covenant generosity that flows both ways. We know people who have much more money but are less effective.

Power to Bless

Exactly how much more blessed is it to give than to receive? I suppose that would depend on how aggressively we give. Covenant empowers us to bless. David said, "Make vows to the LORD your God and fulfill them."[b] Can you see how making a promise empowers you to perform it? If you want to be a blesser, make a covenant with God to be a blesser. And then go out and find someone to bless - He'll hold you to it and He'll back you up.

The un-empowered giver is someone who will decide what to give when the opportunity arises, or they think they will give once their business takes off or when they win the lottery. It never happens because it's not empowered by covenant commitment. Making a vow is to simply make a decision ahead of time; that's what a covenant is, a decision made now about how I will treat you in the future.

All of Both

When God made covenant with Abraham, Abraham became the friend of God. God and Abraham cut covenant father to father. Outside of covenant, if you pick any two people, one is superior and one is inferior in a given matter. But the very essence of covenant is that we become equals, and more than equals, we become friends, brothers. We become 'for the other guy.' The marriage covenant removes superiority-inferiority between a husband and wife, doesn't it. Well, there are many jokes to be told about that, but Jesus describes marriage as a covenant where each lives for the other. In Jonathan and David's covenant, we see how Jonathan gave up his superiority, his right to the throne. Jonathan had what David needed in order to fulfill God's call on his life, so there was an exchange, a shift of commodities. Even God, the creator of the universe, came down and made himself equal to Abraham saying, "As for Me... I give you everything I have," and Abraham replied, "As for me, I give you everything I have."[c]

Any deal made to bring us into submission to a superior or a leader is not a covenant. I've heard leaders complain about an unfaithful follower, calling them a 'covenant breaker.' But a covenant used to make someone submit is not a covenant; it is control, manipulation, witchcraft. If I am looking for an arrangement whereby someone becomes subservient to me, covenant isn't it; I should just hire them. A covenant is not meant to hold you accountable to me but it is my vow to maintain the love that I have chosen to love you with. Covenant is my commitment to love you, not a demand to make you love me.

The Greater Loves the Lesser

As I mentioned, from the book of Hebrews, the greater makes covenant with the lesser, like God with Abraham, and they become partners. I have something to offer those who haven't gone as far as I have in the ministry so in that sense I am the greater making covenant with the lesser. Why? To make them great.

Pastor Peter Jamshed, a former student of our Thailand Bible College was showing me around the great Lahore Fort in Pakistan. We sat down on a bench in the shade and I asked him, "What is it you really want to accomplish in Pakistan?" He thought for a minute and then began a story. "When I was a young Christian, serving God under a pastor who didn't express much love for me or the people in the church...." His voice quivered, "I was feeling very disappointed in the ministry, when one day God showed me that He loves the people of Pakistan." Peter spoke with such conviction that I teared up along with him. Such a simple statement yet such a revelation, "God loves the people of Pakistan." Hearing that come out of this son's heart deepened my love for him beyond what words can express. Getting to Pakistan, because of political complications, costs thousands of dollars each trip and we have to put up with the regular interruptions of suicide bombers and a troupe of armed guards surrounding us wherever we go - yet we go, every year.

The greater initiates the covenant relationship because it is a relationship of love, not of demands. Simply, covenant is a choice to love someone who needs your help. It puts a demand on self to act in love and release, rather than a demand on the other to meet my needs. Covenant allows me to invest my life into my spiritual sons in Pakistan. Amazingly, deep down, we all know that this is what we were made for - to love others who need our help.

(endnotes)

a Deuteronomy 7:9 NIV

b Psalm 76:11

c the story unfolds through the book of Genesis, God and Abraham exchanged their only sons. God put His all into Jesus, everything Abraham had was in Isaac.

Chapter 7

THE LONG ROAD TO COVENANT

The deep kind of roots.

Rich Conte

Back to my story, we had already planted five independent churches. All of our team, people we've worked together with for years, and my wife and I really felt that God was speaking to us very clearly to join Pastor Al and Victory, but we weren't sure about the pastors of these five churches. Even though we were working together the churches were autonomous, in the sense that they were self-governed and self-ruled. So we just came to them and said that we felt like God had spoken clearly to our hearts, to my wife and I, to join Victory and this is the direction that we were going and that they needed to decide if they would come along or if we should part ways. In other words, if they decided to be independent it would be fine so parting ways, but not in the sense that we were in any kind of disagreement. We had always gotten along well and we told them we just wanted them to pray about it. So we gave them five months to pray. My wife and I had been praying for probably close to two years already.

By the grace of God, they all came together and said unanimously, "We feel like we want to go where you go." So I think a lot of it had to do with the fact that we had already built solid relationships with these guys; they trusted our leadership. Of course, they had no idea as to what they were really getting into. I think they just trusted that if we felt that was the direction the Lord wanted, then they were with us.

A Five-Month Decision

I gave them a full five months, because I didn't want them to be pushed into something. And I think if you came up to them today they would all say that they have no regrets. I think they would all say it has been a great life changing decision for them.

Mostly it was just sharing the vision. It's what it is always about, just keep sharing the vision. Of course, they had met Pastor Al. He had come and spoken a couple of times, but they hadn't been to Thailand and seen what was happening there and they hadn't been to Canada to see the Victory organization. So they just had to kind of trust that what I was saying wasn't just hype or fluff. I found that a lot of guys like to be independent and don't want to be under someone's authority. For some reason, they feel like being independent is freedom, but it's just lonely.

I think my guys took a step of faith, but again sharing the vision was huge and I just kept sharing it, especially the vision of reaching into all of Asia. They knew, as Filipinos, that is God's call on this nation. The real question of vision is, "On the strength of five or six churches are we really going to reach a large portion of Asia?" Probably not. So here was an organization that was already reaching into many of the nations that we had a heart for and it was also strategically located. In prayer is where you discern this kind of stuff.

Trust Builds Over Time

If you just keep loving people and encouraging them, they begin to be confident that you want the best for them. Leadership, really, any type of government, is for protection and empowerment - that's the purpose. If you as a leader have that heart for the guys you lead, to protect and empower them, not to restrict or control them, they will begin to trust you. When a leader uses his authority to control people, trust is undermined.

A Nervous Choice

I think any time that you take a step of faith there is a little bit of fear, a little trembling, a little bit of you not being sure if this is really God and what's the outcome going to look like? There's a big risk involved. I think a couple of the guys were concerned about possibly losing their autonomy. Were they going to be able to make their own decisions or were they going to be taking orders that were dictated from somewhere else? Of course, that's one of the great things about Victory; all of the churches and ministries are autonomous. When we come into covenant relationship, we come into agreement about certain things. We come into agreement about vision and about the way we do things, but it is not about control in the way we run our churches or our ministries.

I think that was the main concern. Personally, I don't think I had as many concerns as some of the other guys did because I had spent a lot more time with Pastor Al. I had been to Thailand a couple of times. I had been to Canada and so I had seen the organization. I had prayed longer than they did and I had a lot more exposure and knew a lot more about what I was getting myself into than they did. So I think it was probably fair for them to have had more concerns than I did.

The How To

We got a chance to take the pastors over to Thailand to a Victory Asia conference. That just took the lid off. It was like wow, it's amazing what God's doing here. And, of course, Pastor Al and I continued going back and forth, at least twice a year. He'd come to the Philippines twice a year; I'd go to Thailand twice a year. This not only strengthened the relationships but we saw the anointing on our ministries increase; faith increased and fruitfulness followed. It all just really snowballed.

Nothing wins people over more than success. It's not like we were going after success but an increase in all these things speak louder than any amount of talking that you can do.

A New Way of Thinking

So the decision to work together takes time, but then the shift in thinking can take even longer. Some of the pastors really caught on quickly; others have been slow. One of the things we shifted into was how to think big. So now, we had a handful of pastors who had really caught the idea that we don't have to stay small; we don't have to limit ourselves. That's probably one of the greatest things that Victory has taught us. Let's think big, let's plan big, and several of our pastors have really caught that and they have seen the results in their own churches.

So it was about the time that this covenant relationship was really completely formed when my wife and I released the church we were pastoring and moved into Manila with our core team. We launched the new church with 450 people on the first Sunday and it's grown to 2,000 in 10 years. That was big, considering the biggest of the five churches we had planted before was about 80 people.

Now our Filipino pastors had to make a decision. Was this new level of success because of the covenant relationship we had entered into or was it because I am an American missionary? The answer should have been obvious, but I know some of our pastors struggled with the idea that they could also now do something much bigger than before.

Sometimes you can't avoid that small kind of thinking that assumes the foreigner is more significant or has better chances of success. But some of our Filipino pastors caught the vision for something bigger. As they began to grow and produce more, then the other pastors would think, "Wow, he's a Filipino, if he can do it then I can do it too!" And that's basically what happened with me too when I hung around Pastor Al and saw the things that he was doing. As I spent time with him I thought, "Well, if he can do it then I can do it!"

Chapter 8

A COVENANT NEW WAY

Embracing apostolic ministry.

Rich Conte

Entering into covenant changed so many things. One of the major things that I had learned many years ago, that I had been taught and maybe understood in my head but had not experienced, was the whole idea of apostolic ministry - five-fold ministry. Before joining Pastor Al and Victory Asia, we were barely experiencing any level of apostolic anointing. We had heard lots of talk about apostolic ministry, but on a scale from 1 to 100 we were at a two. Once we connected with Pastor Al and Victory Asia that changed, almost immediately.

There was apostolic anointing and impartation that came, or rather was released. I think that it was actually there all along but had been hidden by our small thinking and we had no idea. It's like the gifts of the Holy Spirit; you know the Holy Spirit is there but you might have no idea how to tap in or how to move into it. Then somebody comes along and just brings it to life. That was probably the major thing, the whole idea of apostolic ministry, the whole idea of five-fold ministry, that we need apostles, prophets and teachers, all of these things, to really function. We knew it in our heads, we knew it in the scripture, but we were only experiencing it in a very tiny amount.

Fresh Revelation

Of course having Pastor Al coming to teach us, just the fresh revelation, fresh impartation, fresh viewpoint, fresh perspective, and those things really changed my life personally. One of the biggest shifts came when I heard him teach on the Abrahamic covenant. I'll never forget it. I heard him teach maybe two or three times on the Abrahamic covenant and then for two years, every time I opened my Bible, all I could see was the Abrahamic covenant. Every page just seemed to speak it to me.

I marveled at the literal promise to Abraham, that his descendants will be as numerous as the stars in the sky, as the sand on the seashore. That whole revelation just took over in our thinking. It became so alive that I started teaching on it. I'll never forget one day, on my birthday, two of my top leaders, without speaking to each other, without knowing what the other was doing, each gave me a birthday gift that echoed that promise. One of them gave me a little plastic bag of sand, and the other one gave me a little bag of glass stars. That was God speaking to me! I was like, "God! This is really going to happen!" So that was revolutionary, the whole idea that we inherit the Abrahamic covenant literally and we can expect God to answer the promises that He made to Abraham, Isaac, and Jacob. We can expect Him to answer those promises for us, today. In fact, Abraham died in faith having not received the promise so we could be the ones to receive it in fullness.

We Won't Go Alone

We actually took all of our leaders by the hand and led them through the process of entering covenant because there was only a handful that really caught it in the beginning. Honestly, it took a couple of years. Again, I think that when they started to see the results, their skepticism left. But the whole thing was really a success because they trusted in our leadership. That trust is what was bringing them along even while skepticism was there. In the beginning two or three of them caught it; now we've got nearly 30 churches and the majority of them are really on board. I think maybe all but about one have fully caught it.

A Shift Over Time

As we brought the subject up at our leadership meetings, in the beginning we had only three or four who were all excited and the rest would be stuck in the old mindset. And then at the next meeting there would be a few more that would join the excited group, and now there is like one guy who everyone else looks at thinking, "You don't get it, do you?" It's a cultural shift and it takes some guys longer, and of course there is the odd one who will never get it and eventually just walk away. Regardless of what anybody else does, I know that covenant relationships in an apostolic company are the way to do ministry that produces phenomenal results.

How to Facilitate the Shift

We have gone through the ten tenets of Victory numerous times and we always come to that one tenet that says, "We have a lifetime commitment to the vision." That's a tough one to accept for some and you can't force them to accept it either. So I don't force the issue, instead I tell them, "You have to know in your heart, you have to hear in your heart that God has spoken to you and this is where you belong." I tell them that my wife and I have made that commitment because we feel that God has spoken to us. One by one we watch them come, but I never force it. Then they'll say, "Pastor, God has spoken to my heart, we're in this for the long term, we're committed for life, we're in covenant relationship with each other." It's not instant, it's a process and I see that little by little the majority of them are working in covenant relationship with one another. We've watched in other places how guys have jumped in and then jumped out just as quickly. We won't do that; covenants are a serious life decision so we promote it. In every meeting we encourage this covenant relationship, not just between me and the guys, but between themselves. We're always pushing, "You guys need to be working together, you need to be exchanging pulpits, exchanging ideas. Whatever strengths this church has, you need to be exchanging with the other churches. You guys need to be cross-pollinating and working together in the understanding that we're all in this together." And by the grace of God that is happening.

Opposite Poles

There is a very big difference between the lives of those you covenant with and those who resist. Coming into covenant relationship really does require a revelation. It's a huge investment you won't be willing to make unless God shows you the potential blessing. When you see it, you can do it; but if you don't see it, then you live like the majority of people who are not in covenant with each other, including church leaders who are not in covenant. When you live independently, you live alone, you live thinking, "I just want to get what I can out of this organization." There's little idea of, "We're working together for a common cause, a common vision."

The difference is huge. Those who haven't really caught it or seen it, they're still on the outskirts looking in. All they're thinking about is, "What can I get? How can you help me?" Instead of, "What can I give? What can I contribute? How can we be together and do something greater?" And likely they will be disappointed in you when they don't get all they wanted. A covenant man thinks differently, he will see a need or a lack and come up with a way to fill that need. A guy who is out for himself will just wait for you to do it and he'll break relationship because he's disappointed that you didn't fill that need for him. When somebody complains, "The trouble with this organization is a lack of..." I'll ask them, "What are you doing to fix it?"

Covenant is a High Calling

When you come into covenant, part of the relationship is that love becomes the covering; love covers a multitude of sins. That doesn't mean that we overlook blatant immorality. It means that if I'm in covenant relationship with you, just like a husband and a wife, we can overlook the differences of opinion. We're not talking about moral issues here as much as we're talking about the differences in personality, the differences in the way that we would do something or say something. Maybe I wouldn't do it that way or say it that way, but we're in this together and we're in this for the long term. Because we're in covenant together I'm not going to let those little things bother me. Whereas if you're not in covenant relationship then all of those little things irritate you, all those little things bother you. Again the trust level is different. If you're not in covenant you are always wondering, "Is he trying to use me? Is he just trying to get something out of me? How can I benefit back?" I keep going back to the illustration of marriage but if you have a good marriage then those issues shouldn't be there. In a marriage gone bad the feelings are, "He's just using me," or, "She's just using me," or, "Is there anything I get out of this?"

That's not what marriage is about. Covenant is about, "We're in this together for the long term. I know you have some weaknesses, I have some weaknesses, you have some strengths, I have some strengths, but we have a future together. No matter what, we're going to make this work. God's called us together and we stick it out." This kind of trust is the foundation of covenant.

Chapter 9

COVENANT'S NEW BLESSING

More than we could ask or think.

Rich Conte

Once we joined Pastor Al and Victory Churches International, things really took off. We went from our five little churches to planting the one in Manila with 450 people in the first service. That was our sixth church, it was our turning point. Attendance shot up and we quickly planted another church. As we planted churches, those churches began to plant other churches. This was a totally new rate of growth. In our pre-covenant days it took us 17 years to plant five little churches. Since we've gotten connected we've enjoyed planting another 20 churches, larger sized churches in shorter time frames.

Here is a really good illustration: one church that I planted in the old days, opened on the first Sunday with 8 people. It took 15 years for that church to finally become self-supporting; we had to financially and physically keep the thing afloat for all those years. Once we joined Victory that church became completely self-supporting, they have a gorgeous building, and they have planted two more successful churches. That's just the tip of the iceberg. I am always amazed at the level of anointing that can be released and the exponential growth that can happen when you come into covenant with apostolic leaders.

Growth brings new challenges. Growth is more than just a greater volume of the same old thing you had before, but growth means we develop new skills, new resources, and most of all, a new mindset. Not only must we increase in the number of leaders we have, but these leaders must have greater capacity and capability. One of the greatest challenges we faced was to re-train our old leaders and break some of the old mindsets. They had to understand that the new increase we were enjoying was not because we had joined a big organization that was now pouring resources into the Philippines. That's the wrong mindset and it's simply not true, and if it were the case we would just be living under a new ceiling, one that was higher, but a ceiling nonetheless.

In order to flourish, our leaders needed to understand that the growth we were seeing, the multiplication we were experiencing was because of an anointing that had been released. It's simple enough to say it's the anointing, yet until you experience it, it's not so easy to understand or believe.

Many people think growth will come by successfully applying this program or that one, or if somebody gives them money. The fact is, and I am emphatic about this, our growth has happened because there has been a release of apostolic anointing into our team. Getting people to understand this has been a big challenge. They see what's happening and they'll say, "Well, now that Pastor Rich is connected with a big organization, he gets funding..." but it's just not true. God's Spirit is the real agent of change and we are growing as a result of the apostolic leadership and anointing that He has brought us into through these covenant relationships.

The real challenge is to raise up enough capable leaders, great people capable of exploits, who can go with us to the next level because as Dr. George Hill says, "You have a whole lot more opportunities than you do qualified leaders to fill those opportunities." This is a constant challenge.

But Now We Have Help

When you're in covenant relationship you have people you can go to who have actually gone through the challenges that you're going through. They can give you good and godly advice that has been proven to work because they have been through the exact same things. The wisdom we glean from them is essential to growth. You can read the same stuff in books and for some reason it doesn't click. But once you've built a solid relationship with someone and they tell you, "This is what you need to do in this situation, this how it happened with us," you find you can do it and it works. The difference between being in covenant relationship, especially if you're in covenant with people who are ahead of you, is that the anointing and wisdom flows down to you. Then it's not just head knowledge, it's imparted, applied, and the coolest thing is that it actually works.

Crisis Recovery

Now that we've experienced covenant, the idea of being independent seems like a nightmare. Entering covenant relationship didn't stop bad things from happening, but now we had the support of a really big family. A few years ago, that same church I planted with 8 people some decades ago, burned to the ground. The building was an old wooden structure. The neighbour's propane bottle exploded and both their house and our church burned right to ashes. Everything was gone. So of course we wrote to VCI and told them what had happened. They immediately took up an offering and raised, if I remember correctly, $10,000 to rebuild that church.

The guy who was pastoring at the time made a wise decision. He decided they would take the $10,000 and build as much as they could of a two story solid concrete building. That kind of money doesn't go very far; it got them the basic ground floor, enclosed but not finished. But the structure, the steel and such, was in place for the second floor and they figured they would just finish it off as they could raise the money inside the church. I wish you could see that church today. It is gorgeous, one of our nicest looking churches. Victory came to the rescue but didn't give us all the money, which was a good thing. If somebody had given all of the money then the local congregation wouldn't "own it." So over time the church just kept putting money into the building, and now it's a beautiful, air-conditioned building, and they've planted two flourishing churches out of it.

Without that kind of family help, we probably would have had to rent a place because we had no finances to begin rebuilding. I'm sure the church would have survived as far as being a church, but to see the building now, I'm incredibly proud of it. The $10,000 Victory gave us was seed money that got the rough first floor up. That gave the people enough hope and faith to build the rest of the building themselves, and they did an amazing job. They probably invested another $30,000 over the next few years.

This crisis followed by the way the greater family responded, really helped unify and inspire the congregation; they all got involved whole heartedly. They saw that we care! It showed that this organization actually cares about us. It's more than just talk.

Chapter 10

COVENANT STRUCTURE

Covenant gives things a proper shape.

Rich Conte

The way you structure a ministry, or even a business for that matter, plays a big role in its success, and in its rate of success. A wrong structure can hinder growth just as a proper structure can facilitate growth. The first big challenge is to form one structure that fulfills two separate purposes: to meet secular government requirements while facilitating the Kingdom vision of the ministry. It can be like trying to mix oil and water, especially in countries where they make no allowance for Christian objectives.

We also need our structure to facilitate change and growth. In many organizations, structure has become a hindrance to growth, slowing decisions and resisting new vision.

Our Structure

We have the legal structure in place as far as names and positions go. We have several boards of directors: we have an international board, a provincial board, and we have a metro Manila board. Each local church also has its own board. We have it all in place legally but we don't really function by board control. We set direction by knowing our purpose, casting vision and then working together through relationship. When you say the term 'board' it inspires a picture of a bunch of guys sitting around a table. You can call us a board but we function as a group of friends who love each other, while we're working together in covenant relationship. Sometimes we hold regular meetings, sometimes we have emergency meetings, but we're pretty well all in agreement before we even come together because we are following the same vision. When it comes to making decisions, we not only want to know what each person thinks, but we also want them to carry the weight and responsibility of what we decide as a group. For our ministries to be effective, we can't have guys who sit on a board just to make decisions and then won't do the actual work or help pay the bills.

Again, trust is what makes covenant relationships so powerful. If you have a board of people that don't trust each other then you're going to end up in arguments because you don't trust the motives of the guy across the table from you. But in covenant relationship it's like family. You know that everyone sitting at the table actually has one heart, one mind, one agenda. When we're building God's Kingdom, we want what's best for the organization and we want what's best for everyone, then we don't suffer under a lack of trust. It's a whole lot easier to solve problems that way. Fixing things still takes time and energy, but we're doing it together.

Eliminating Divisions

In working together in any group it is important to eliminate the attitudes that segregate and divide. Covenant has the power to do that. Let me illustrate this. One of the things that really drew me to Al Purvis was that he really did the same thing I did, even though he was in Thailand and I was in the Philippines. When Pastor Al came to Thailand, he joined the Thai society. He learned the language, he dressed Thai, and ate Thai food. He has always viewed and treated the nationals as equals. That doesn't happen in every missionary organization, unfortunately. I have been on the mission field for over 30 years and I have witnessed far too often how foreign missionaries have come in and kind of lorded it over the people, like they're the big boss and the people they come to minister to are somehow lesser.

Al and I had the same mindset; I did the same thing he did. When I arrived in the Philippines I lived with Filipinos, ate with Filipinos, I actually had no communication with foreigners at all for many years. My leaders were Filipinos, so I adopted their language, their culture, their ways etc.... Pastor Al did the same thing. That was one of the first things that really clicked when it came to building this relationship.

I am still American, and I still have some of those American quirks and weaknesses,; though there are plenty, we won't talk about those even though they still come out. We've spent the necessary time and have enough of a track record with our Filipino brethren to have gained their trust. Little by little we have involved more national leaders in the decision making, treating them as equals from the very beginning. All of us feel that we are truly working together in relationship.

In contrast to that, there are some mission organizations in which the nationals actually resent the missionaries and I've heard them say it on numerous occasions. Nationals resenting a missionary is a pretty sad thing. He's probably a guy who has sacrificed, come to another country, and he's a messenger of the Gospel, yet the very people he is trying to minister to really resent him. A lot of it is his fault because he's treating them as if he's the big white boss and they're the national natives. His condescending attitude of, "I know better than you," builds resentment.

Covenants function on love for the other party. If we truly love the people we've come to minister to we will respect their worth in God and treat them as we would want to be treated.

Again, the purpose of leadership is protection and empowerment, not control. If you are genuinely pouring into people's lives to empower them to become better, to reach new levels and become more successful - if you're really doing that, then it doesn't matter who's white or black or Asian, it just doesn't matter.

Racism is Baser

Racism is firstly a result of personal ignorance and secondly a result of the ignorance of leaders. The colonial mindset of an organization produces the same attitudes in its missionaries. For example, many organizations will have a compound where all the white missionaries live and the only natives allowed inside are the maids and the janitors. How are you going to reach the people from that lofty position? So if you're a new missionary on the field and you have a heart for God and a heart for the gospel and you've joined this organization, you'll end up being like the organization.

I was really influenced by Hudson Taylor. If you've ever read his biography, that was exactly his situation. He went into a mission organization like the one I described, and those types of organizations still exist today. Hudson Taylor built a new organization, not like the colonial model. He aggressively opposed that model. He went to China with an organization that had a compound where all the white people lived and he just said, "This is not the way to reach the Chinese." And if you read his biography he left the organization, dressed like the Chinese, ate what they ate, learned their language, learned the ways they lived. He ended up planting thousands of churches across China and being responsible for bringing thousands of missionaries into China. He led hundreds of thousands of Chinese to Christ because he became Chinese.

One of the problems is that the colonial type of organizations are structured so that the missionary is told what to do, where to go, and worst of all, what he cannot do. That's control isn't it? That's the big difference between apostolic covenant relationships and a typical organization or denomination. Not that every organization or denomination is like that, but unfortunately there are many that are. Orders are dictated down through the ranks of hierarchy and there's very little relationship. That level of control tells me that there is a lack of trust. The reason an organization would dictate what can and cannot be done is because they don't trust that their missionary will do the right thing. But in covenant relationship, even though we all think somewhat differently, even though we come from different experiences, we know each other's heart. When we know each other at a heart level we trust each other with the freedom to make decisions. It works because we've spent time together.

It's the same thing with my pastors. I don't dictate to them what materials to use and which ones not to use. I have built enough of a relationship with them that I know that they're not going to do something weird or crazy. We give them freedom because freedom fosters growth. But when you're controlling people, when you're dictating everything to them, you're actually stifling growth, you're stifling ideas, you're stifling creativity. And then you'll say things like, "But we've been here 30 years and this is how we've always done it."

Accountability Counts

In many organizations accountability is kept by filling out forms and reports. But when you're in covenant you're kept accountable by relationship. When you actually have a relationship with the person you're in covenant with, spending time together, they can ask you tough questions and you're not shocked or defensive because you have given them the right to ask you tough questions. Husbands and wives have the right to ask each other tough questions because they are in close relationship with one another.

Effective accountability comes with covenant relationship. Accountability is not just a way to control wrong actions but an empowering of right actions out of a healthy heart.

We do use forms and those kinds of tools, but real accountability happens far more on the personal level of, "How are you doing? What are you struggling with? What's happening? How are your finances? How are you handling this problem?" There's a lot more personal interaction than just filling out a form. In fact, forms hardly guarantee honesty; people can put anything on a form. But if you're in covenant relationship you can tell if somebody is lying or failing in some other way because you know them well enough. So you can interrupt them and ask, "Really? Is that really what happened?"

It comes down to this: family. The church is supposed to be family, really. We've strayed from that, especially in North America, but in other parts of the world too. "Church" is not defined as the activity of coming to a building on Sunday, singing some songs, hearing some guy give a message, and then going home not knowing anybody. That's not the church. It's about family and it's awesome to be a part of the family.

Covenant relationships are meant to be mutually beneficial to both parties, not just one-sided. If both parties agree, then both parties give and both benefit in the relationship. The Bible tells us that two have a greater reward for their labor than one. Jesus tells us that if two of us agree on earth as touching anything, it will be done. This is a powerful promise, directly from Jesus, that agreement releases things that are otherwise unattainable.

Chapter 11

FRIENDS BECOME FAMILY

Covenants build relationships.

Rich Conte

There are three requirements of covenant: 1. Loyalty regardless of circumstances, 2. Truthfulness regardless of cost, and 3. Forgiveness regardless of the pain. That's how families are meant to treat one another.

The covenant between Jonathan and David exemplifies a bond in brotherhood that we, as believers, are meant to join together in. Jonathan and David had a bond that was stronger than the connection between blood brothers. Jonathan's covenant with David greatly strengthened David's vision and his resolve while he faced attacks from the power hungry and crazy, King Saul. Jonathan was able to stand and protect David, helping him escape from Saul on several occasions.

Even though Saul was his father, Jonathan made a covenant with David that meant he was willing to put himself at risk for David, and give up his own right to succession as king. Jonathan saw by faith that the future of the nations was with David. This covenant had massive repercussions! David would become the king of Israel, fulfilling God's promises to David, the nation and to the world. King David was called and anointed to establish the throne and the bloodline of Jesus the Messiah.

Isolation is a trap of the enemy! We were meant to be in covenant relationship with one other because there is great power and protection in such a relationship. The devil knows this. He actually understands the power of covenant, so he'll do anything he can to keep that from happening. An isolated man or woman is easy prey for the enemy.

Covenant's Inferiors

Covenant is not merely a partnership, it's not about networking with people, it's not just friendship, and it's not a tool for helping one another out. All those things are good but they are limited. Networking is a good thing, but what networking says is basically this: "You help me a little, I'll help you a little; you give me a little something, and I'll give you a little something." But there's no real binding commitment, nor any submission of authority or accountability to one another. It's, "I'm still independent, you're still independent, we're networking, and we're just helping one another." And most friendships are basically the same thing. There's no power in a relationship like that. Of course you stand to benefit a little, both parties may even benefit somewhat. But the power, anointing, and destiny that can be transferred via covenant relationships will never take place through networking or partnerships or even close friendships.

The fulfillment of the prophecy of Jesus' lineage today is a strong testimony to this. After David came his son Solomon, a man of incredible wisdom. Solomon built God's temple and wrote the book of Proverbs, a book that greatly impacts people even today. Steven K. Scott is a successful businessman who decided to read a chapter from the book of Proverbs every day. He did that for more than two years and went from being a man who failed at seven jobs and two businesses to become a multi-millionaire. The wisdom he gained from the book of Proverbs allowed him to co-found the marketing company American Telecast. Thousands of other businessmen, both Christian and non-Christians alike, have followed suit by incorporating principles from the book of Proverbs into their business policies.

The point being that today we are still walking in the blessings and success that were provided for in the David-Jonathan covenant of brothers. All of these blessings could have easily been missed had Jonathan not protected and promoted David. So many people's lives have been blessed and continue to be blessed by Jonathan's faithfulness to that relationship. And in return, Jonathan's family and even those who worked for them were greatly blessed as well. Your covenant brothers and sisters will open the doors for protection, support, and immense blessing not only for you but also for those who come after you.

The covenant bond concept lifts a friendship like this to great heights, as a covenant not only gives you a partner who will stand in the gap for you, keep you accountable and lift up your dreams, but you will also have a relationship that God blesses with His power and support.

Empowered by Others

A covenant of brothers paves the way for your brothers and sisters to encourage and empower your destiny. The covenant connection drives a person to strong focused prayer for their covenant partner. That prayer covering releases God's power and frees Him to enact His perfect plan.

A common attitude towards prayer that we find in the church is that we ask others to pray for us, perhaps concerning a trial we are facing, or whatever. The person will nod sincerely and promise to pray. They will then go home, face all kinds of immediate needs, get dinner ready, notice the leak in the bathroom, work on their job report, get sucked into a television program, intend to respond to only one person on Facebook and then spend the next couple of hours looking at friend's pictures! The intention to pray is there, most people honestly do care about what others are going through. Still there is not that same connection that pulls at their heart and creates the urgency and determination to pray, to pray like you would for a family member. Covenant changes that.

The disconnect in our commitment to pray is connected to the intimacy level of our relationship with that person. As harsh as it may seem, the likelihood of us going home and spending hours in prayer over a stranger's request is pretty small. Yet if your own child, your spouse, or your best friend came up to you and told you that they had just been diagnosed with a terminal disease, not only would most of us easily go home and pray for them continually, but we would also stop right then and there and pray for our loved one.

We have trained ourselves in a world of so much hurt and so many problems to just tune it out. That news report about massive famine in Africa may pull at your heart, but it will be your ailing grandparent in the hospital that your mind will go back to, because they are a deeper part of your life. Having a covenant brother or sister creates a greater covering between the two of you. What tugs on your heart will draw on theirs as well. They see your vision as a part of their vision, what you love is what they love; you stand for and fight for the same ideals, the same goals. As you join in prayer together your hearts will be focused and each side becomes more accountable to pray for the other. The power of the prayer of agreement cannot be over-emphasized.

Inheritance

Every action we commit in our lives will have a great impact on the generations to come. Conversely every inaction can and will be just as important. Today the Middle East still reels under the effect of Abraham's decision to try to fulfill God's promise on his own, creating the violent debate over the proper lineage of Isaac and Ishmael. Many of the things we do in the here and now will affect the lives of our children and beyond, whether good or bad, so it's up to us.

Any sane parent would want to leave an inheritance of blessings for their children. There are enough hardships in life that they will have to face so why not try to help your children where you can? You are not going to be able to be there for them all the time, your hand of protection can only reach so far. Thank the Lord that He is a God of covenant, a God of relationship! Because of His commitment to us we know that He will continue to be committed to those who come after us as long as they walk in covenant relationship with Him. Likewise we can open up ourselves and others to equally blessed and beneficial relationships. God's covenant with us will transcend generations. A covenant of brothers can and will do the same.

One thing I've learned in being connected with Pastor Al

and Victory Church is how to think big. Whenever you get around people who are thinking big that tends to rub off on you. Not only have we been taught how to think bigger, we have been able to teach the people under us how to think bigger. When we talk about covenant relationships and inheritance there can obviously be transference of ideas, and even transference of anointing. There are so many natural and tremendous benefits we receive from one another because of being in relationship that can be gained no other way than together.

These benefits of genuine covenant relationships cannot be over emphasized: protection, participation, prayer and intercession, but the greatest benefit of all has to be the transference of anointing. I am convinced this transference happens only through highly committed and proven relationships, like the relationship between Elijah and Elisha, Paul and Timothy, and Jesus and His disciples. There is a lot more than just teachings or principles being transferred. There is power!

Chapter 12

COVENANT EXCHANGE

True generosity.

Rich Conte

Pastor Al and his ministry team have invested a lot in us. They send workers, they send equipment, knowledge and expertise and they take time with us. They spend time with us because it's a long-term commitment, a family-like commitment. You would never think twice about investing into the lives of your children because they're your children; they're part of your family. Covenant is not about 'give and take,' it's about 'give and give,' and reaping a harvest of the true benefits of giving.

In covenant relationships, we freely give to one another. What's yours is mine and what's mine is yours. A few years ago in our church in Manila we were in great need of a media producer. Pastor Al's nephew, Chris Kaptein, was well-trained in media and had worked producing television commercials. He was probably the most important media guy Pastor Al had in Thailand when the Holy Spirit began to speak to this young man to come help us in the Philippines. In our covenant relationship there was absolutely no hesitation whatsoever on Pastor Al's part. He immediately released Chris to come and he came for three years. I know in the natural it must have felt like a big loss for the ministry in Thailand because Chris was such a key guy in the production of their new TV show, Continuum. Though Chris was their best editor and their best camera man, Pastor Al released his best without hesitation. That's what covenant relationships do.

On the other hand we had a wonderful couple in the Philippines, Ronald and Cynthia. Cynthia was my right hand. She was my administrator and I depended on her for everything. Ronald was like my left hand. These were two of my best workers and they felt God calling them to Thailand as long-term missionaries. Again there was no hesitation. There was no, "Well, we need you here." Covenant relationships provide a free flow of exchange because in the spirit of covenant what belongs to you belongs to me, what's yours is mine and what's mine is yours. There is a covenant level of generosity between people who are building God's Kingdom rather than doing their own thing. There are a lot of leaders that, if you asked them to release their worship leader or Sunday school teacher would respond with, "No way!" They're not going to be that generous because they are fighting to build up their own end of the ministry. In covenant relationships, not only do we release but there's no hesitation or second guessing or after thoughts. "Well sure, of course!"

Giving Destiny

Jonathan understood that David was to be the next king of Israel and initiated the covenant between them that would bring the plan to fruition. This covenant meant that Jonathan would give his right to the throne over to David. In the story Jonathan's unselfishness is described as, "He loved David as himself." He gave David everything that pertained to becoming the future king. Jonathan took off his robe and gave it to David, along with his tunic and his sword, his bow and his belt."[a]

Jonathan's robe was his royal garment, representing his position as prince and heir to the throne. The things we exchange in covenant are the most valuable things we have.

Once again, while David was at Horesh in the Desert of Ziph, he heard that Saul had come out to take his life. Jonathan secretly went ahead to David and encouraged his covenant brother to be strong in God. "Don't be afraid," he said. "My father Saul will not lay a hand on you. You shall be king over Israel, and I will be second to you. Even my father Saul knows this." The two of them made a covenant before the Lord.[a]

Covenant simply doesn't work for people who aim to gain more than they will give, which is a totally wrong understanding of the purpose of covenant. What we give in covenant isn't just people, or money, or other material things. We give success, destiny, even legacy.

What I Have is for Both of Us

Making a covenant means we are willing to give up what we have rights to, similar to Jonathan giving up his position as heir to the throne. Why would he do that? He recognized God's anointing and calling on David to be the next king. Only a pure heart after God could even conceive of such a self-defying vision. But Jonathan believed that in covenant they would rule Israel together. Both David and Jonathan cared more for the nation of Israel than they did for themselves. They didn't care who got the credit, they just wanted to do their part to see God's Kingdom come. Saul was the opposite.

In this covenant, Jonathan was more loyal to David than he was to his own father! Godly relationships within the church can bring you into conflict with your own relatives and then we have to decide where our loyalties lie.

When Jonathan gave David his armour, representing his covering and his protection, he gave up his self-preservation. Relationship at the level of covenant requires openness, honesty and transparency, as well as a departure from self-preservation. I speak the truth in love, not only about you but about me. "Faithful are the wounds of a friend, but the kisses of an enemy are deceitful."[c]

Truth is in the Token

The covenant act of Jonathan giving David his weapons was a promise of two things: 1. These weapons will never be used against each other and 2. David could now count on Jonathan to fight for him, not against him. I love that scene in action movies where in the middle of a struggle, the good guy hands the bad guy his weapon and the relationship instantly turns 180 degrees, from trying to kill each other to trusted friends fighting together for a common cause. It always begins with the ultimate risk of, "You can kill me if you want to."

The Broken Ones Don't Covenant

If covenant gives success, destiny and legacy to others, what kind of people are eligible for true covenant relationships? Covenant demands healthy people. Do you know anybody who married an emotionally or spiritually broken person? How did it turn out? It is so very important to be healed and whole before entering a covenant. David said he hated the lame and blind. He meant that he hated his enemies who had no sense of honour or integrity. They were spiritually lame and blind and could not be trusted. They were not capable of living in covenant.[d]

What about Jonathan's son, Mephibosheth? He was lame. His physical lameness did not offend David. He loved the crippled son of his covenant brother, and moved him into the palace to live and eat with the king. David honoured and extended his covenant with Jonathan to include Mephibosheth, even after Jonathan was dead. But Mephibosheth was incapable of entering such a relationship of trust; he was emotionally lame as well and the covenant couldn't fix that. He foolishly betrayed David one day when it appeared that David would be ousted from the throne. He had a deformed hope that in some lame way, he would become the next king of Israel. David responded by giving everything Mephibosheth owned to Mephibosheth's servant. The goods are always looking for faithful men.

Broken people tend to think, "If I can just marry the right person, or meet the right friends, or live in the right place, or find a better job, everything will get better." There's not much chance of that. Covenant is not where we go to get good things from others but where we give the good things we have to others. This requires emotionally and spiritually healthy people.

For the broken, healing is available even when you've been hurt and disappointed by what you once believed was a covenant relationship. In order to fulfill God's call on our lives we need to come to a level of spiritual and emotional health where we can drop our defenses as Jonathan and David did and trust each other.

Covenant puts us into place where we belong, which is

diametrically opposed to rejection. Covenant gives our life worth which overrides low self esteem and covenant establishes competence in contrast to inadequacy. If any of these are missing we will have difficulties making genuine covenant relationships.

(endnotes)

a I Samuel 18:1-4

b I Samuel 23:15-18

c Proverbs 27:6

d II Samuel 5:8

Chapter 13

COVENANT PROTECTION

The act of protection.

Rich Conte

As Pastor Al and I have built this relationship, of course it flows down from the fathers to the sons. He has covenant relationships with other people and so do I, for example people I work with. In the Philippines we have strong covenant relationships throughout our ministry. When Pastor Ezekiel Pudpud went out from our church to plant another church, we sent ten families of our congregation with him as a core group. Not only did these families have great potential as leaders in our own church but they were also among our top givers. But they lived 45 minutes to an hour away from our church and we felt that the new church was a better fit for them. We also believed that Pastor Ezekiel was capable of planting and pastoring a good-sized church. We released those people without hesitation or second thought. Our own church offerings dropped significantly for several months because of sending away some of our big givers, but the principle of the Kingdom is that you will reap what is sown. So if you sow givers you are going to reap givers. It took six or eight months, but now giving has increased ten-fold in our church.

As time went on, Pastor Ezekiel's church ended up renting a large facility. The congregation was growing, but they couldn't really make the rent payments and they were getting more and more behind. When Ezekiel came to talk to me about it, I believe they were four months behind. We're talking about a lot of money, roughly $20,000 in the hole. That is a lot of money. For a third world country it's a huge amount of money. At the same time a group of his leaders rose up against him and began to prophesy bad things about him and the church. They gathered a group of people around them and split the church, taking six of his top leaders and 25 of his people. About that time the landlord of the place he was renting chained and locked the door and cut off the electricity. The people who split off from the church had prophesied that, "If what we're doing is from God, this church will collapse. If this church does not collapse then we haven't heard from God." It looked like they were right!

The story doesn't end here because Pastor Ezekiel and I are in covenant relationship. He is a man of God and a man of integrity even though he is in a desperate situation at this moment. And no doubt a split could be avoided by not promoting immature leaders too soon.

Covenant relationship means that you rush to protect the one that you are in relationship with. Ezekiel came to us and we immediately began to send people and finances. I personally began preaching in the church weekly, bringing teams, laying on hands, bringing the fire of God, and bringing revival to the church. We continued this intense level of help for a good six months. We also loaned them enough money to pay their outstanding bills. Now they are completely out of debt, they have 700 people, the church is absolutely rocking, they're going through revival and they have new facilities. They are happier and better off than they could imagine. That kind of change is what covenant relationship facilitates. You support the guy that you are in relationship with.

Pastor Ezekiel may have made some mistakes, but he certainly did it innocently and there was no lack of integrity whatsoever in his life. He had made some commitments financially that they were unable to fulfill, but he had moved ahead with a word from God, and he had a family that he could turn to when he was in trouble. Had we not been in covenant relationship that church would have certainly closed; I have no doubt in my mind that that church would be gone today. Now if you were to visit you would find this church totally on fire. In covenant relationship we defend and protect our brother.

Covenant Protection Gets Personal

One time we took a bunch of our pastors from the Philippines over to Thailand for a conference. We were at the airport in Bangkok on our return to the Philippines when this unscrupulous Filipino man approached our group. He was trying to get all of our team members to take his large boxes back to the Philippines as their personal luggage. Well, I'm hesitant about the whole thing because we have no idea what's in those boxes. There are a lot of innocent people in Asian jails, caught carrying a suitcase for someone else that was found to be full of drugs. He claimed that it was something like flowers. This Filipino guy was a total stranger and he wouldn't take no for an answer so I stepped in. I'm the only American in the group, and he gets heated up. He's angry at me for interfering. He's a big guy for a Filipino and I'm small for an American and he's demanding, "Who are you? You're just an American. I'm talking with my Filipino friends here."

Antoinette, our chief intercessor, has been with us since she was 15 years old and so she is like a daughter. She stepped in between me and this big angry guy, ready to start swinging. She was so defensive and so protective of me, I'll never forget it. It was like, "Wow, this girl would really defend me and protect me." The obnoxious man walked away shaking his head. The idea of a Filipino girl defending an American guy in an airport was probably inconceivable. That is a covenant relationship. That's part of what Jonathan and David were saying by exchanging their swords and their weapons. They were saying, "Your enemies are my enemies. I'll lay down my life for you; you'll lay down your life for me." Again it's not instant but it is built over time. You would be willing to take a bullet for the person that you are in relationship with, and you will end up protecting your covenant brothers and sisters. That's true covenant relationship.

Big Boys Need Correction Too

Covenant relationships release greater success into our lives, and greater success requires greater responsibility because the chance of failure increases along with the greater success. I've noticed that men or women who get off track do it while believing they have all the protection they need in place. Rules concerning the opposite sex and the handling of finances don't seem to guarantee safety.

Covenant relationships offer a more powerful protection against moral failure than policies do, if these relationships are really close. When we feel a responsibility toward someone we will ask them, "How is your personal life, your devotional life, your marriage?" Al and I challenge each other, even in the little things, to be diligent and effective, to keep our hearts right and pay attention to anything that could be the one weak link or pillar that gets knocked out causing the building to collapse.

I wonder if David would have avoided committing adultery with the beautiful woman he saw bathing on the roof if Jonathan had still been around. A big part of the problem was that David had no peers and he had no leader, nobody to tell him to get out there and lead his men in battle. The only person who could speak into his life at that point was Nathan the prophet, and he had to do it by telling stories. Jonathan would have held David to their covenant purpose: David was to be the king, not an embarrassment to the nation.

Chapter 14

COVENANT ADOPTION

How to become a real family.

Al Purvis

Terry and I adopted 27 Thai children and called our big family, 'The El Shaddai Family'. We also had four children born to us naturally so that made 31 in the family.

One of our adopted daughters Jaruny came to me one day when she was in her early teens and needed a ride to school. We lived in a town on the gulf of Thailand where our home was about 4 kilometers from the school, so I would take her on the back of my motorbike. When we made the final turn toward the school, she tapped me on the arm and said, "Dad, I'll get down here." That was strange because I had to go as far as the school to make a u-turn anyway. Then it dawned on me that she didn't want her friends to see her foreigner father - there would be lots of questions. In true fatherly fashion I drove into the school grounds and paraded once around just so she would have to deal with it. The hurtful part was that we had raised this girl from a young age and only two years earlier when she was deathly sick in the hospital, I drove that same bike two hours each way through Bangkok traffic to visit her every day. So it's not like we had neglected her.

Before she finished high school she asked if she could transfer to a special college. It would cost us more money but we wanted her to have every good opportunity. That was about the last we saw of her. She met a boy who got her pregnant, beat her and abandoned her. Now she works a dead-end factory job to feed herself and her son.

Our son Neo, actually the same age as Jaruny and born in the same jungle village, was attending the same high school. On a similar day he needed a ride home. On the phone he said, "Dad, bring the big bike, my friends want to see it." High school boys would be impressed by my tired out 750 cc Suzuki, kept alive with Yamaha and Honda parts. When I turned into the school yard I could see Neo running towards me from four buildings away. He jumped on behind me and told me to drive past the sports field; his teachers were out there preparing for a track meet and they all got a royal wave from this proud teenager on the back of his dad's motorbike. Then we had to drive past four buildings to, "Pick up my schoolbooks." The whole thing was staged; he had 20 friends standing there holding his schoolbooks and when we pulled up he announced with pomp, "This is my dad and this is his bike!"

The only difference between these two kids was 'adoption.' We had adopted them both, and loved them, but only one of them had adopted us back.

Adoption is a process made up of choices, and the right choices end in covenant relationship. During our engagement, Terry and I adopted each other as husband and wife and then cut a covenant on our wedding day that signified we are one.

The process of adoption happens through excitement and

hardship, receiving something and committing to something. For Rich and I and a family of leaders across Asia and other parts of the world, it's the forming of friendships where communication changes from, "Hi, how are you? I am fine." To, "Check out this new software, here's the link." Or, "How should I deal with the critical talk between some of my leaders?" Or, "How are we ever going to pay for this?"

Adoption requires revelation, something that takes place in the heart, not just in the mind. The mind is great for doing business, it comes up with ways to benefit through certain relationships. But covenant happens in the heart.

Adoption Goes Through Steps

The first step is to recognize a kindred spirit. A kindred spirit according to Webster's Dictionary is, "An individual with the same beliefs, attitudes or feelings as oneself." Anne (of Green Gables) was always looking for people who were of a 'kindred spirit,' a term she probably learned from Isaac Watts who referred to a kindred spirit as a 'pure spirit' in his 1753 writings.

Often when we meet new people our first impressions are clouded with preconceptions and with what's going on in our own brain. But when we are in such a state of mind as to put love first, we will meet people through purer eyes and possibly recognize a kindred destiny in them, a same vision. When Jesus saw Nathaniel coming He said, "Look, an Israelite in whom there is no guile!"[a]

The second step is to recognize a role we might play in their lives. When we first met Rich and Ning, they were obviously very tired, and because we saw no guile, arrogance, or agenda in them, we wanted to bless them. That's what they saw in Terry and I in turn. So for me, their tiredness and the possibility that we could encourage them became the preview of a possible destiny together. We weren't looking for destiny or a connection, we just saw an opportunity to encourage some unthreatening people.

The third step is to form a relationship around the right thing. When I first met Terry, I was very impressed by her passion to serve God. We worked together in an evangelistic team and decided to become a couple one day during a communion service. Our first date was our honeymoon. Our relationship was formed around vision first, romance followed. Don't misunderstand, you can't have a marriage without romance and we can never get enough, but our future is determined by what we build our relationships on. The power of our marriage relationship has built ministry in a bunch of countries. We have a growing number of covenant relationships built around Jesus' commission to make disciples in the nations.

The fourth step is to grow the relationship by doing the right things. This is investment of the rarest kind, and a return not produced by what we might gain in a win-win relationship, but by giving to better another. This requires confidence; I have to know that I have something amazing to invest in you that will make you better.

The overarching point of a covenant relationship is that we continue doing the right things, even in adverse or costly circumstances.

The Higher Call of Covenant

One of the first things Rich ever expressed to me was how he disliked the very popular idea of networking. It's not that he didn't desire to work together with other people but that networking is shallow; it's a level of commitment that goes only as far as what it will cost me to get what I want from you. I've always felt the same when someone mentioned a 'win-win relationship,' another popular idea. A relationship built on mutual benefit is a lesser relationship since it is measured by the amount of personal gain. A covenant relationship is a spiritual relationship for the reason of benefiting the other, towards a greater purpose. We were created in the image of God to be like Him, loving and benefiting others. When God said, "Take dominion over the earth," He didn't mean a dictatorship. He meant we are to spend our lives protecting and blessing the earth and its inhabitants. With this others-focused motivation, we're not just trying to get along and get what we can. Instead, we'll actually fight for peace because we hate war and we'll punish offenders because we hate the way they abuse the innocent. We'll act for the good of others.

Covenant is where we live above, on a level higher than win-win or networking; covenant takes authority over selfishness.

(endnotes)

a John 1:47

Chapter 15

MAKING COVENANT REAL

Covenant is not make-believe.

Al Purvis

Our team was in Vietnam ministering in a conference for leaders of the underground church. Over two hundred leaders stuffed themselves into a living room; they were probably the hungriest people for God we have ever ministered to. Many wept and praised God as the Holy Spirit revealed the power of apostolic ministry. We were interrupted by the police halfway through the conference and deported from the country. But before we left, a group of leaders asked me to become a spiritual father to them. With considerable sadness I had to say no. These were our brothers and sisters, kindred leaders, but because I simply couldn't be there for them, I couldn't play such a serious role in their lives. You can't be in a real working covenant relationship if you're not there.

Pastors who think they are in covenant relationship with some national leader on the other side of the world are just kidding themselves, unless they are spending a lot of time together, working together through the challenges of ministry.

I get a kick out of missionaries who will say, "That guy is my spiritual son," but they can't even pronounce his name. I've heard pastors claim that some very well-known Christian leader is their 'accountability pastor' yet they've only met once or twice in conferences and have no ongoing two-way communication. Covenant for covenant's sake is not our goal. What we want is the level of relationship that covenant represents. A covenant is not a badge of coolness for Christian leaders; it is a result of building a relationship for the right purpose.

Make Yourself Friendly

If you are independent and tired of it, the first thing you need to do is make some real friends. Find someone who needs your wisdom, authority, and resources and begin to bless their life; begin giving to them. Or, if you have lots of friends but desire some real solid covenant relationships, do the same thing. Begin to give what can't be repaid. Remember, this will never be about what you can get, but about what you can give. Covenant is where the greater gives to the lesser, so start giving in the areas where you are stronger.

I encourage all the guys on our team to share the information that is most valuable to their success and the success of others. When you know something that the others don't know it puts you ahead in the game, right? Well, give that information away to help the other guy get ahead and the whole team gets ahead. Hoarding information or knowledge is a sin. If you're a dog in a dog-eat-dog world, you had better keep all good information to yourself. In fact, if you leak wrong information you can even trip up the other dogs. I would hate to live in that world.

In our ministry culture, if one leader reads a good book we all expect him to share the best things he learned with the rest of us. That way each one can read a different book and share the best truths from them. As a team we can end up reading a number of good books every week.

Make Yourself Useful

Because covenant relationships are always formed around a purpose, you need to do something useful; build something, create something that will benefit others. Take on a project by your own initiative, facilitating and empowering advancement for others. Every leader and every team is looking to recruit people who can do things. Some guys don't catch this very simple key to success: people who can do things are people who have done things. And people who can do things are in high demand.

A musician in our worship team who can play more than one instrument and sing well will be scheduled for the worship team far more often than someone who can only play the tambourine. And for those who can't play or sing at all, we encourage them to worship with the congregation.

I estimate that during the first 20 years of ministry I learned about one new profession every year. Of course you don't become the best at every single thing, but it's a big fat lie that if you are a jack-of-all-trades you end up being a master of none. If you can do many things you become much more useful to others. An added benefit is that in leading the ministry now, I don't have to believe it when I hear, "Oh, that can't be done." Because I can tell you how to get the proper reports out of the accounting system, or how to wire a three-way switch, or equalize a sound system, edit a TV show, preach a sermon, mix concrete or rebuild my Jeep. And I love leading a team who can do many of these things better than I can plus a lot of things I can't.

Barbecue

This is the solution to everything when things aren't moving ahead like you want, or relationships are strained, or just need to be recharged: food is the answer. My wife can cook! (If you need some inspiration, get her book "Cooking Thai with Terry.") We've never had relationships go wrong when there was food involved. This runs deeper than taste buds. In probably every culture, you are not really friends until you've eaten together. Eating is deeply relational. Some of my kids even post photos of what they are eating when they go to a coffee shop. They want the world to know, "Me and my buddy had an awesome piece of cake together in a cool place."

Being invited to eat at someone's house or function is an honour. This kind of honour is a covenant response that we have encountered from Pakistan to the Philippines. In some of the smallest, poorest homes, we have eaten king's fare because it's the best way a host can find to honour someone important to them. Sometimes there are gifts, plaques, flowers, songs, and things, but food is always there.

Eating together is a covenant act, sealing and deepening relationships. Jesus held a last supper for His disciples. We still receive the bread and wine today that Jesus calls, "The new covenant...." And we eat it together. I mentioned that my wife and I decided to become a couple during a communion service. What better way to foreshadow the life-long covenant we continue in 35 years later. A real covenant relationship will continue to grow and deepen.

Covenant Really Happens

In marriage there is a wedding celebration and in church membership there is a ceremony of recognition. These are wonderful celebrations but the actual covenant being celebrated is formed over time and has many steps to fulfillment. Rich and have I never actually said, "Let's make a covenant," but over time we have gone through the steps that form the covenant relationship. You probably have lots of covenant relationships that you may not even realize are covenant relationships until you stop and think about it, but they are. In most cases covenant relationships come together without documents, signatures, or tokens; you don't even have to cut your finger and mix your blood. Covenant relationships are effective because they have taken place in our hearts, are sealed in prayer, and have been proven over time.

Covenant really is a natural result of pursuing God's purpose and loving His people. Once you have that happening, people will be drawn to you. If you're self-centered and critical you don't have any friends who would die for you and you're the only one who can fix that.

Chapter 16

COVENANT COMMITMENT

God's Covenant Plan.

Al Purvis

A visitor once asked me, "With over 30 kids, can you really remember all their names?" Yes I can, and I tuck every one of them into bed at night.

When our family had grown to 17 kids, I told Terry, "That's the right amount, that's enough." But how do you tell an orphaned kid, "No, we don't have room for you." So we grew to 31 and then started another home that grew to 20-some. I wish we could stay young forever because the jungles and slums are full of kids who need a good home.

But 'capacity' is a legitimate issue and there is a limit to the number of hours in a day and money in the bank. Being committed to 31 kids was a full-time job - that's how we did it - full-time. When our oldest girls were in grade four the teacher asked the class to write down their dad's profession. We had three girls in that class and they whispered to each other, "What does our dad do? He's not a doctor or a businessman or a fireman." So they wrote down, 'Nothing.' When I picked them up after school they asked me what I did as a career, and

I told them, "I am your full-time father." Just driving them to and from school took four to eight hours a day in the Bangkok traffic of the '80's.

The Measure of Commitment

We always loved having visitors come from North America or Europe to visit our El Shaddai Family home. They would come and fall in love with our kids because they were so cute and funny. And many of these people became our best ministry supporters when they saw what God was doing in the lives of these kids. A story of a kid being rescued from desperate situations will always captivate the hearts of caring people.

On occasion our guests would initiate this very solemn conversation, "We've decided we want to adopt one of the kids. How do we go about it? We can give her a good home. She'll have every opportunity for a great future. We've just fallen in love with her and feel she'll be the perfect addition to our family."

"Hey! These are our kids, get lost!" Okay, I've never said that, because I fully understand the attraction. But I could have easily been offended at the suggestion that our level of commitment to these children was less than that of our guest's. We are spending our lives to provide these kids with a good home, an education and every opportunity for success. We were certainly the more genuinely committed. But the argument in my head could never convince anyone against their own feelings. I needed an answer that could be felt.

So my answer was, "Sure, you can have one of my kids. I'll trade you straight across for one of yours."

Another question often asked was, "How long do you keep these kids?" Again, my answer, "How long do you keep yours?"

Commitment doesn't come by the kilogram. People only understand commitment by measuring it against their own level of commitment in an area.

People who have never walked in covenant relationship have no way of knowing the deep joy of such a level of commitment. It's like durian, the king of Asian fruits. Folks who've never tried it think they know what it's all about. Banned from public places because of the pungent odour it emits, it's often dismissed before it's tasted. But once you've savoured the right mouthful, you'll be hooked. If you approach Durian with preconceived disdain, you'll be one of those who condemn it as unfit to eat. My wife doesn't allow it in the house so I eat it in the back yard. Once you've experienced the joy of covenant commitment and the fruit of its success, you'll be addicted.

Assessing Capacity

Our ministry mandate is to make disciples across Asia. As we train and mentor an increasing number of young men and women and send them back to their nations, our commitment to help them succeed also increases. We promise to travel to their country every year as well as host them in Thailand for ongoing training and vision casting. We are seeing ministries flourish in nation after nation across Asia, and now beyond. But where will it stop? At what point do we reach our maximum capacity? How do we measure our potential capacity? Does this train have any brakes?

Truly, there's no way I can squeeze more hours out of a day

to make new commitments to new sons and daughters - there is a physical limit. What I am about to say has to come by revelation, not that it's deep. Quite the opposite, it's way too simple for most people to grasp

Rich and I have just increased our capacity by writing this book. I know lots of people have written books, most of them have little to say. I get that from statistics: the average sales of every book ever written are 200 copies. Subtract all the million best sellers and that leaves most books having practically zero impact, because they have zero substance in a world where people need real answers and powerful inspiration.

There are relationships that have zero impact, zero substance, because there is no commitment, no giving, no sacrifice and no genuine love. When I say zero, I mean there is probably an immeasurable amount. It's immeasurable because the person has no scale to measure commitment. They don't grasp or understand the substance of covenant because they are self-centered. Moses was like that for the first 40 years of his ministry. He and God were arguing over whose people the children of Israel really were. God said they were Moses' people and Moses insisted they were God's people. Neither one wanted them because they were more trouble than they were worth. Commitment is always more trouble than it's worth, if you're measuring the wrong thing. Finally, Moses laid down his life for his brothers like Christ laid down his life for us, and then he experienced the love of God. Moses' words were no longer accusing the people but he had joined himself to them and prayed, "God, we are a rebellious people, please forgive us and go with us...."[a] Now he was a leader for the right reason.

A book written for the wrong reason becomes pointless. A

relationship entered for the purpose of receiving rather than giving ends in disappointment. Becoming a leader just to appear successful will only wear you out.

People often tell us, "You guys have done an amazing job in raising all those kids." And we appreciate the compliment; however, true or untrue, God knows. It's good to recognize accomplishments, but if we begin to do things for the purpose of being praised, then we'll be living life with the flesh side up.

Like the many books that are written with nothing to say, there are many relationships that hold no commitment, and promises that have no integrity.

Here's the Bottom Line

If in a selfless state of heart I can conceive the value of a commitment to serve others, I'll join up, like Moses did. It's not about my success, except for my success in empowering others into their Kingdom destiny.

Now I See

When Moses got it right, he was able to successfully lead over a million people. I don't think he knew all their names but they certainly knew his. Commitment in covenant relationships results in an ever-expanding level of influence. 'Greater influence' should be defined as the ability to move people more effectively toward their destiny with less effort. By increased influence we can lead more people. Remember that influence doesn't come from setting yourself up, or working your way up some hierarchical ladder or landing a position. True influence is born out of commitment.

To someone on the outside this may look like smart people growing a ministry that can attract a large following. But on the inside we know that our commitment and sacrifice attract people of kindred convictions willing to commit to each other through mutual adoption.

Our capacity of 17 grew to a capacity of 31 and now to hundreds of successful leaders working together in covenant relationships for the sake of making disciples across Asia. The key to increase isn't to learn how to divide our hours between more people or become more efficient, although those are legitimate skills. The key is to include more people and that requires a commitment to the destiny of more people. So it's not about how many hours in a day, it's about how committed I am to seeing others succeed.

Understanding covenant takes the lid off your capacity.

Back to writing this book, Rich and I simply want to share with a greater number of people how covenant relationships can empower greater success. And now that we have these ideas in a book, even more people can be blessed and our capacity to influence has increased.

(endnotes)

a Exodus 32:7, 11, 32, 34:9

Chapter 17

INCREASING COVENANT

Moving on to greater exploits.

Al Purvis

I came into Christianity out of a hippie lifestyle. I owned an old car and a couple of guitars and I had no job or job qualifications. To my good fortune, Terry agreed to marry me but then supporting her became my responsibility. I received a phone call from a company in another city offering me a permanent job, complete with training, a company house, a real car, a good wage and benefit package: all too good to be true. This looked like God's answer for my new life with my new wife, but out of my spirit came, "No, thank you." We learned to trust God by other means.

Companies offer such great deals to get you tied in as a career employee. The cost of upsetting the work crew and training new technicians outweighs the cost of the benefit package that keeps you loyal to the company. Smart companies use ever-increasing wages and benefits to hold employees fast. The longer you stay, the harder it is to leave.

Likewise, a covenant between brothers is strengthened as the benefits of the covenant increase. Over time the commitment, honour and friendship develop to add value to the covenant. Each succeeding benefit shared between brothers adds strength to the covenant in the same way as a scale of benefits keeps employees faithful to the company. The longer my brothers and I work together in Asia and the more of the Kingdom we build, the more reason we all have never to quit. We are shareholders, owners of the same purpose. When I receive a phone call offering me a better ministry package it's easy to say no, not because the offer is bad but because I don't want to start over at zero.

Reset to Zero

Leaving a covenant relationship will reset my influence and my spiritual benefit package back to zero. And worse yet, it sets a precedent for quitting whenever things don't go my way. I've never done it and I never will. When a family moves to a better church they must begin to build their influence, ministry and relationships again from zero. This may sometimes seem necessary but the more you do it, the less Kingdom you will own in the end. Jesus is going to reward us for our share of Kingdom influence and advancement, not for our number of new starts.

A Precedent to Success

In 1981 we landed in Thailand as new missionaries, but we had more than one country in our hearts. We settled in Bangkok, learned the language, raised a Thai family and founded a new ministry that was reaching out on several fronts. But how do we reach the next nations? Should we move to Vietnam, learn the language and launch a new ministry? With that kind of math we might be able to minister to three countries in our lifetime, one at a time.

What if we never ever quit anything or any place but expanded through annexing the regions beyond to what we had already built? That's what the Apostle Paul did.[a] Through a series of very difficult events and keeping a right heart, we ended up with a five-storey building on the eastern seaboard south of Bangkok and needed something to fill it with. A simple idea dropped into my heart. Why not fill it with students from the other countries? Places like Vietnam, Laos, Cambodia, Burma, and throw some westerners into the mix too. It was just another one of those ideas that people responded to with, "Oh, that can't be done. Those are poor countries, they can't afford to travel and they won't be able to get visas to stay here…." No problem, we'll use our faith! We've trained leaders from 16 countries so far and have already expanded the ministry, not to three countries but ten. And our horizons are just beginning to look big.

So the principle is: don't start over in Vietnam, but expand from what you've already built in Thailand to include Vietnam and a bunch of other countries. All you need is covenant relationships. Anybody can make covenant relationships; it just requires commitment to empowering others to succeed.

A New Opportunity

In the beginning of our relationship, Rich was really attracted to the idea that we could work together to reach all of Asia. This was his vision too. Rich and Ning knew they were standing on the threshold of a big move forward and began to pray about moving to Thailand and becoming part of our core team. The churches they had planted in the Philippines all had good leaders in place and were able to support themselves now. Moving to Thailand would be an exciting fresh start for this tired couple, but on second prayer, it would be like leaving the foundations of their calling in order to take the next step forward. It just didn't sit right. So they shut the door to that idea and began to focus on rallying the leaders and churches they had already planted. We are all so glad they did, because what God has done through this couple in the Philippines has become one of the greatest success stories of our relationship and a wonderful model of ministry for our other nations across Asia.

Too often we watch people make the wrong move forward, abandoning the great investments of the past for some new opportunity that presents itself as the 'big one.' That may be how personal fortunes are sought but it's not how kingdoms are built.

This is the first key to success: never reset your life. And it looks like this: Terry and I have never left a church or a ministry.[b]

The Second Key to Forward

Don't just give a man a fish, teach him how to fish. It sounds good, but in fact, most of them know how to fish and they just don't want to. And you can invest a lot into teaching people something they'll never make a commitment to. We meet a lot of people who want to connect with us. Usually they come looking for us when they hear that we are in their country. They are looking for something and it is often presented as the 'teach us how to fish' thing. So during our first conversation, I tell them we want 10% of anything they catch.[c] Wow, that's a shocker! But if you are not willing to commit 10% to the success of this ministry, why should we commit 100% to you? Mission organizations would save millions of dollars if they would work through proven covenant relationships rather than those unproven relationships that are built on the exchange of money for notoriety. Shallow leaders will pay big dollars for the appearance of expanding their ministry into new countries. They hold the recipient accountable by requesting reports, then at the point of highest payoff somebody will run off with the money. Real relationships cost commitment; that means sacrificing together and then winning victories together.

The strength of a covenant of brothers is built through difficult front-line advancements, including some close calls, and winning for each other. The battlefront can be over external things like acquiring land, buildings and equipment, or internal things like standing for each other through criticism or leadership politics. Covenants do not have an expiry date because they are based on love for the other guy and there is always a way we can make the other guy better. So when things get tough, covenant shines. Rich and I are committed to this covenant because we have gone through some things together. Our past victories paint a vivid picture of what our future can look like.

Driven By Inferior Desire

Potential missionaries stay home for fear of missing out on the American dream. Middle-aged pastors quit in fear that other opportunities are passing them by. Professionals switch professions and spouses change spouses in efforts to gain a better life. I know every one of us have our own story of why, but Jesus said that in seeking a life of benefits we will lose it. The way up is to give it up.[d] I wish these resets were the exception to the rule, but they are far too common in the world and in the church. We're not looking for a new start, but to reach new areas and new people by standing on what we've already accomplished.

Influence and Legacy

Consider past heroes, men like Wilberforce, Edison and Churchill. There is a long list of heroes but they are a small percentage of the population in their times. We won't talk about today's leaders because they won't become famous until their shortcomings are forgotten and only their accomplishments are remembered.

Heroes became heroes because they held to their convictions, honoured their family and friends, kept a singular focus, and did it all against great odds. Most are remembered for one great achievement. Unending resolve is the trademark of greatness, but resolve ceases to be resolve when the reset button is pushed.

Many of us have experienced a forced reset by lay-off, divorce, or accident. Most successful people have been forced back to zero more than once. Several times, Terry and I raised resources for the ministry in Thailand and then lost it all by the hand of someone who shared our space but not our purpose. This is an innocent reset: our bank balance went back to zero, but not our resolve. We never quit. A voluntary or intentional reset is a fail: we can't win because we don't fight.

Can you see the difference? Outside circumstances may do their level best to send us back to zero but if our heart does not give in, those challenges become food for our purpose and we move forward. But if we abandon our commitment to push forward, it's like we're wasting all the things God has brought us through in the past to prepare us for the greater future. We each have to figure this out for our own lives. What might look to be a setback is actually meant to trigger a launch forward. If we diligently keep our heart right and stay in faith, we will end up with a new level of blessing every time.

There is a way to discern and manoeuver such changes so that the trip meter doesn't get reset to zero, but in my experience, a small percentage of leaders actually move in continual increase.

Covenant Reveals

If your covenants are not broken, neither is your life. Covenants between brothers will protect us from the mistake of quitting and starting over again from zero.

(endnotes)

a II Corinthians 10:13-16

b In 1985, we were asked to leave our original sending church when there was a change of pastors, otherwise we have never knowingly broken fellowship with anyone.

c In Victory Asia, local churches tithe to their national headquarters, the national headquarters tithes to Victory Asia, and Victory Asia tithes to Victory Churches International. On every level, the more we grow, the more empowered we are to grow even more. There is no ceiling.

d Luke 17:33

Chapter 18

COVENANT ACTION

The honourable act honourably.

Al Purvis

Covenants are necessary only because our world is hostile to God and contrary to our good. In the Garden of Eden, covenant had no role to play, until the serpent showed up and man's honour was lost. Covenants are God's arrangement to bring honour back, restoring the goodness intended in the original creation. God made man in His image and saw that it was very good.[a] God honours the man who calls upon Him.[b]

But honour is a shy substance, many times disguising itself as humility or hiding behind the scenes while the honour that takes the stage often lacks the substance of the real thing. Real honour isn't looking for a stage; it's looking to pick a fight with injustice.

During the early years of our ministry, a friend came from Canada to visit us. We enjoyed her company and proudly showed her around the ministry in Thailand. Then as we drove her back to the airport, she confessed, "Actually, I was asked to come here by my leader to find out what you guys are really doing over here, and my report won't be favourable." We escorted her through check-in, waved good-bye with a smile, and then we dropped into the airport lounge chairs like a couple of rag dolls. At that present moment I felt emasculated, incapacitated and incapable of even driving home. Her opinion of our ministry wasn't a big deal; we had heard lots of criticism. Her coming as a spy wasn't the worst thing, although it's difficult to be a spy and friend at the same time. But to have a ministry leader send someone to spy on us? That was sabotage. You will never follow a leader like that because it is mathematically, scientifically, and grammatically impossible to honour someone who is dishonourable. Dishonourable means 'can't be honoured.' A couple of hours later we drove home and resumed our lives.

The way David honoured King Saul is often cited as an example we should follow in honouring anyone who is in a position of leadership. But I have studied that story in detail, and the prayers David prayed. He prayed that God would take Saul out.[c] David honoured the office of king that Saul occupied but he never honoured Saul's foolishness or selfishness. He ducked, he ran and he prayed against him, but he wouldn't touch him. He left that part to God alone.[d] David truly was honourable, but he didn't honour Saul and he didn't follow him. The nation hated Saul and God rejected him as king. Honour does not excuse evil. Elijah didn't honour Jezebel, the queen of Israel, who was subversive, intimidating and a manipulator.

Source of Honour

Honour takes place in real life, often unnoticed by the public and not scripted. It comes straight from the heart, according to what's in there.

WW II German fighter pilot, Franz Stigler, forfeited the highest medal for bravery his country offered and risked being shot for treason when he came across an allied bomber shot full of holes and barely airborne. He offered to escort his enemy to a safe landing in Switzerland rather than shooting him down. He could see the Americans on board desperately trying to save their wounded brothers. Stigler learned honour from his commander, "If I ever see or hear of you shooting at a man in a parachute, I will shoot you down myself." It was lodged in his heart.

Honour has rules, not policies, but core beliefs that tell our hearts what to do. Honour comes from having a common enemy. In WW II, inhumanity was a common enemy. For the honourable, human dignity was of even greater importance than the war between the Axis and the Allies.

Honour Rises

If you attack my brothers you become an enemy to us both, and in honour I will execute justice. Honour acts on behalf of the other guy, many times by simple, powerful words that defeat an attack. Have you ever heard that someone defended you against criticism when you weren't there to defend yourself? When someone else defends you, how many times more powerful is it than when you defend yourself? But it's not about the value of you; it's about the value that honour places on truth.

We are in a war over honour. Like blood diamonds in Angola or drugs in Burma, self-serving leaders have put a price on honour. They want it. Honour is a commodity that can finance their agenda. Honour is the currency of influence. If I honour you, I will please you, follow you and obey you. You can control people who honour you or you can empower them for their destiny. That's why there is such a battle over honour. In Thailand the royal family is honoured and revered above all else. What begins in the nursery as, "Never step on a coin or any other insignia of the king," becomes the loyalty that kept the country from falling when communism was dominoeing its way across South East Asia at the end of the '70"s. Honour controls masses.

Have you ever been the target of a love stalker? It's creepy and it's the opposite of love. "You need to honour me" is similar; it's the same creepiness because it's a manipulation to hold power over you that you don't want to give. True honour, like true love, must be mutual. Honour is meant to be the currency of covenant, not the currency of manipulation.

Stand Apart

Covenant men are a different breed of men and honour is our superpower. We live where honour trumps agenda, honour beats criticism, honour lacks personal ambition and honour protects the vulnerable. Honour is the virtue that sets us apart from the masses and makes me a significant soul. And honour lives well in obscurity until we are needed, and then does what's right even though it's impossible. Men like Cincinnatus of Rome, Churchill of England, or Stigler of Germany are honoured for their one-off acts of courage that saved the world or at least inspired us to be better. But they got there by being honourable consistently, when no one was watching.

A Culture of Honour

In the world the loser honours the winner and the humbled

honours the proud, even if only theoretically; but in covenant, honour goes both ways. "A man's pride will bring him low, but the humble in spirit will retain honour."[e]

The patriarch Jacob's last words concerning his sons Simeon and Levi were, "Let not my honour be united to their assembly."[f] He did not want his reputation to empower them because they were murderers. Honour means keeping our nose clean from the dirty business of other men, even if they are closely related to us.

There's a lot of talk about honour these days. Such an important part of personal integrity is to know what and how to honour. What will you fight for? I will stand and fight for my conviction that you are called to a great destiny.

Not Every Cause is Honourable

Men can be joined by honour or divided by honour, depending on what they stand for. If we stand for the cause and commandment of Christ, we stand for the value of every lost soul and the potential of every disciple. In our vertical covenant, we stand for loving God with everything we have; and in our covenant with brothers we stand for doing to others as we would have them do to us. If you stand for these, it is my honour to walk with you, and if you don't stand for these my honour will not allow us to walk together. Paul said, "Do not be unequally yoked with unbelievers."[g] Opposites don't have any fellowship or communion.

(endnotes)

a Genesis 1:31

b Psalm 91:15

c Psalm 143:12

d Psalm 17:2

e Proverbs 29:23

f Genesis 49:6

g II Corinthians 6:14

Chapter 19

LET'S WALK TOGETHER

Walking in honour.

Al Purvis

About 1983, I wrote down the dreams of my heart and ended my self-exhortation with, "We will walk in love and mercy." We were in Thailand, devoting our lives to a war against the principalities of this world. But there was another war to be fought, an equally passionate war against the intolerable offence and division that can happen among believers. We were stunned at the squabbles and criticisms that festered in the body of Christ and determined that we will walk in love and mercy with all.

As new missionaries we often heard from our seasoned brothers about what couldn't be done here, and particularly that Terry and I would be the ones who couldn't do it. I was maverick enough to do it anyway but I felt for the young guys who believed these old guys and often ended up returning home discouraged. I made up my mind that I would never discourage a dream, especially the ones that sound impossible.

I can actually imagine myself as a guy who gets the credit 20 years later when I hear, "You're the one that encouraged me." The real honour isn't in the accolade; it's in my conviction that everyone's dream is a pearl of great price.

My Conviction

From its genesis, our world has suffered the tyranny of self-appointed, self-serving rulers that devalue the rest of humanity. Tyranny thrives on the mindlessness of the masses, the lack of purpose of the multitudes who are trapped in an ordinary existence. Sure, in my world and yours, things are not like that at all. We have the conveniences, technology and opportunities to do about anything we wish. But when we step out of our 8% world into where the other 92% live, what do we find? Hopelessness has settled over their enthusiasm like cardboard shacks over a garbage dump. Every person living in those shacks has dreamed, at least once, that he could do something worthwhile, yet the circumstances of his life have relegated him to an ordinary existence. Another problem with ordinary men is that success can easily turn them into tyrants. A true hero could not be scarcer than he is today. Honour was lost in Eden but Jesus brings it back.

Honour Brings Men Back

Ordinary men have tried to accomplish the extraordinary by outright will-power and failed, or by unified power and failed, or by staying power and failed. In other stories, these virtues may be considered the secrets of success, but I beg to differ.

The truths revealed at the end of an accomplishment might not be the ones that empowered it in the beginning; they are just the outcome or the hindsight. However, there is an underlying truth, a bottom-line secret code that we begin with. Honour will empower our dream and hold us to our destiny. Honour is invisible to the ordinary eye, unnoticed by the masses, attracts only the humble, and inspires only the faithful. Honour can call a person out from the multitude and turn them into a hero like it did for Daniel, David, or Deborah.

This priceless code of success is the straight truth of what God believes about Himself, what He believes about you, what He believes about your world, and what you believe about all that.

Honour at the Heart

Honour at the core will bring forth honourable words and actions. When I believe what God says about Himself, and about me, and about my potential, then I can be that guy. It's simple really, put honour in and you get hero out.

We put honour in with, "Let the word of Christ dwell in you richly in all wisdom, teaching and admonishing one another in psalms and hymns and spiritual songs, singing with grace in your hearts to the Lord."[a] And, "Let your speech always be with grace, seasoned with salt, that you may know how you ought to answer each one."[b]

It's been said that our missionaries never raise their voices in a disagreement because we've become so Asian. That's not true. It's because we don't have to.

We have a simple plan to build honour from the inside out. In our covenant team we are committed to speak a common language, the language of Jesus. We speak and act in love and mercy because the devil wants us to speak criticism and harbour offence.

How to Act

When Jesus says, "Do unto others as you would have them do unto you," He makes the assumption that we know how we want people to do to us. To make the golden rule work in covenant relationships, just think about what those things are and write them down.

Here's what honour looks like in our ministry culture across Asia:

- Honour doesn't exaggerate the facts to make us look better nor does it use our resources to buy fame.
- Honour doesn't diminish or limit others or act in jealousy, but provides a way forward for others through generosity. Jealousy comes before a fall.[c]
- Honour doesn't plagiarize intellectual property or claim credit for the accomplishments of others but gives credit.[d]
- Honour doesn't gossip, criticize, or berate, but encourages and praises. Criticism comes before a fall.[e] Criticism and gossip are the language of betrayal.[f]
- Honour doesn't belittle, berate, or threaten, but supports individual creativity and finds a way forward for the team.
- Honour doesn't hoard but releases with delight.
- Honour doesn't hide behind fig leaves. Honour would rather be forgiven for mistakes than cover them in denial or in blame of others.
- Honour judges us with equity and despises being abused by Saul or Jezebel.
- Honour honours every person and the anointing on their lives.

Where did this list come from? We learn these things from Jesus but it was Saul and Jezebel that brought them to our attention. If you haven't run into Saul and Jezebel, you will if you are on a quest for honour.

When Saul or Jezebel tries to diminish us we rejoice because God is the only one who could actually diminish us, and He doesn't. We turn their belittlements into opportunities for advancement. I wish I had time to tell you of the lands and buildings and promotions and relationships and equipment and voice and influence we have gained by holding to honour when these two attacked. Bring it on!

Increase in Honour

True honour takes two, whether man and wife, father and son, or covenant brothers. We develop in honour together. Honour requires conviction, commitment, correction, humility and encouragement. It requires that we do life together for a purpose greater than our own. As iron sharpens iron, so a friend sharpens a friend.[g]

As we spend time together honour is built. It is my great honour to spend my life with covenant brothers and sisters in nations across Asia and around the world. I am always better for it.

David describes the man of honour: "Lord, who shall abide in your tabernacle? Who shall dwell in your holy hill?

He that walks uprightly, and works righteousness, and speaks the truth in his heart.

He that backbites not with his tongue, nor does evil to his neighbour, nor takes up a reproach against his neighbour.

In whose eyes a vile person is condemned; but he honours them that fear the LORD. He that swears to his own hurt, and changes not.

He that puts not out his money to usury, nor takes reward against the innocent. He that does these things shall never be moved."[h]

Honour is the unwavering decisions you've made to be that guy, the one Jesus said knows how to act toward others.

(endnotes)

a Colossians 3:16

b Colossians 4:6

c Proverbs 27:4

d Proverbs 31:31

e Proverbs 16:18

f Proverbs 11:13

g Proverbs 27:17 NLT

h Psalm 15:1-5

Chapter 20

COVENANT ELEMENTS

Getting the right results.

Al Purvis

A covenant between brothers is a powerful relationship. And given that it is founded on honour, let's move on to the working requirements of the horizontal covenant.

Who is My Covenant Brother?

You can't make a true covenant with just anybody. Here are the three basic requirements:

First, we must have the same proven purpose. I love to meet people who believe what I believe and have the same passion against the same injustices we see in the world. We've built our team by bringing such people together. Together we discover our corporate destiny.

Having the same purpose is an obvious requirement, but nonetheless quite rare. A lot of groups form around a common purpose but then don't last because they just thought they loved the same purpose. We meet as strangers and none of us are so much the same that we'll naturally get along, so it's not easy. Purpose must be proven by sacrifice and investment before it produces the passion that will overcome all differences. I need to know how imperative this purpose is to me and to you. When Rich and I came together we both had about 17 years of purpose-proving prayer, trials and successes behind us. That experience not only proves the purpose but brings value into the relationship.

Value can come by other processes as well; it doesn't have to take 17 years. Peter Jamshed came from Pakistan to study and be mentored by the ministry in Thailand and, more importantly, to get connected to us. It cost him and his family nearly everything they had, including leaving his wife and children at home so she could work and support the family. Their level of sacrifice showed the level of passion with which they were prepared to pursue this purpose. Many others from across Asia have come in similar ways, all making unbelievable sacrifices for something that has about as much visible substance as a daydream.

When we recognize a true purpose we will be willing to invest everything we have.

Secondly, covenant requires a full sacrifice. Have you ever been part of a fund-raising campaign that called for 'equal sacrifice'? What a great biblical idea. Making covenant is similar, but calls for 'total sacrifice.' Can you find the humility to offer everything you are and everything you have to someone else who needs it? Actually you can, because covenant runs a lot deeper than just giving stuff up.

Imagine this, Terry and I meet Rich and Ning in a time and place where all four of us are about done for. We were really tired and not knowing how to get from where we were to where we dreamed of being. That was the first thing we had in common. But that dream is just as alive in tired people as it is in young people or old people or any another people with the odds stacked against them. Rich and Ning impressed us as really nice people so we talked to them and found out they were doing the same things we were doing, totally different experiences and different understandings of it, but the same vision: planting churches and training disciples. We had no plan other than to be friendly, yet we sensed a glimmer of hope that God was orchestrating something great for us. Then God spoke to Rich through prophetic words. Moments later I prayed a prayer out of my tired heart and God released His Spirit, laying Rich out on the ground by the pool. At this point in time, all of us had nothing to lose because we just couldn't go on with things as they were. We could have put all we had at each other's feet and it wouldn't have made a very big pile. The problem comes when we think we're a big deal and we can't see that what we have right now isn't the dream come true. It never is, it's just the seed looking for the next field to be planted in.

A covenant becomes a new field for a greater dream, if we're smart enough and brave enough to plant it.

Covenant requires full sacrifice, full risk and our full attention.

Thirdly, covenant will only work between people who can get along.

I wish I could save leaders from the heartbreak of broken relationships because they can knock the wind out of your vision. A string of broken relationships can embitter you. Broken ministry relationships are common simply because people can't get along once the honeymoon is over. Being in covenant together requires that we know how to be nice to each other.

For many people the biggest consideration when entering a covenant is the risk to their ministry or identity, or whatever is valuable to them. But in those things God guarantees a great harvest on what we have sown. What isn't guaranteed by God is our ability to get along. We'll have to set up our own guarantees for that one, hence a covenant of brothers. In covenant we pre-determine how we will maintain the relationship and how we will act; not like two business partners who used to be friends, but like brothers who can continue in a healthy relationship.

Getting along is not that hard. Just do the right thing, and doing the right thing springs from honour. It works in marriage, with our kids, our friends and in the workplace. Have you ever had a co-worker who acted ugly to you yet nice to certain others? People really do have the power to be nice when they want to; there is no valid excuse for being hard to get along with.

I don't think I've ever had or heard an argument among our team of strong-minded leaders who minister across Asia... and we spend a lot of time in very close quarters. Yet I know other leaders who are so prickly and contrary that it's hard to be around them - and that's not only inexcusable, but an unnecessary destruction of relationships.

When David finally became king of the entire nation of Israel, every single person loved his leadership. They say you can't please everybody, but David did. He did it by honour.

The story goes that Joab, David's army general and long time friend, had killed a man - actually murdered him. The guy he killed was an enemy during wartime but the war was over and Joab couldn't let go of the grudge he held against the man. Maybe it was somewhat justified, the man had killed Joab's brother during the war.

The way David handled the situation revealed his sense of justice and honour: killing an enemy in wartime is fair, but killing the same man in peace time is murder. David made Joab get down and mourn for the man he had just killed and the entire nation followed David in mourning this man's death. It was David's equitable decisions and orders that the people followed. The story says that, "The people took note of what David did and everything he did pleased them all."[a] We want to be in covenant with leaders who lead for honour, not convenience or for a personal agenda.

I might believe I am leading with a pure and honourable heart, but unless my words and actions are boldly honourable, I'm not genuine and people will not follow. So maybe being nice isn't so easy after all. If you're not sure about how to 'be nice,' re-read chapters 19 and 20, and study what you can about honour. Study the life of David from the books of Samuel, his attitude from the Psalms and his understanding as he passed it on to Solomon in the Proverbs.

People will not follow a leader if they feel they're being used for a personal agenda nor will they keep a good relationship with a brother who is not honourable. The men and women I get to hang out with in our ministry are the nicest people in the world.

(endnotes)

a II Samuel 3:36

Chapter 21

COVENANT EXPECTATIONS

It's about what I get to give.

Al Purvis

One of my spiritual daughters was engaged to a man who began the relationship as a gentleman but became very controlling. When she started having second thoughts, the guy told her that their engagement was an unbreakable covenant and that she had to marry him. Because of her honour, she felt bound to follow through. This guy's manipulations were a big red flag that a life of abuse was in store for this sweet girl.

Because of her sense of honour, telling her, "Don't do it," wasn't good enough, so I used the law of Moses to bring a release to her thinking. If engagement is an unbreakable covenant, which it's not, as a dad I had the authority to break it and it would not affect her honour.[a]

Let's unscrew the screwed up thinking that allows manipulators to manipulate others in the name of covenant.

God calls His covenant with us a 'covenant of love.'

A contract or agreement is based on honour, and that's why a handshake is often all that's required to seal such a deal in a society that upholds honour. A covenant is a commitment to love. It's active and ongoing. Honour is what we believe about ourselves, love is how we act because of it. A covenant will fall back on honour if godly love stops working, but then you'll notice a big lack of 'nice.'

We don't enter covenant for the sake of honour; we enter because we love. Our marriage covenant is not based on honour; it's based on love for the other. We promise to love the other until death parts us. Honour shows love how to act and how to love unselfishly.

God gave us a list of filters to discern and succeed in knowing true covenant love.[b]

Generosity Filter

Covenant love gives to one another without begrudging or controlling. If I give money to a man in Laos and then watch to see if he uses it properly, I don't have a covenant relationship with him. I have a relationship controlled by money.

Money is a big revealer of the thoughts and intentions that are hidden in the heart. The way people discuss and make financial arrangements reveals exactly where they stand with you. Money flows very freely through our ministry covenant relationships. We love to give. In covenant we become giving oriented rather than receiving or withholding oriented. I've carried amazing offerings from some of our poorest countries to other countries in Asia. We are the only missionaries I know of whom often come home from poor countries with more money than what we took in. Every nation gives to all the others because all of us love with a spirit of generosity. That's why God blesses us with buildings, vehicles and equipment as well as great relationships.

Empowerment Filter

Have I ever felt a twinge of jealousy against Rich and his amazing ministry in the Philippines? Impossible! It would take a warped man to feel jealous over the success of his brother or his son. Jealousy simply doesn't exist in covenant love; it finds no source and no place. The bigger Rich's ministry grows, the more fun we all have. How about Joseph from India who came to study for two years and returned to open a Bible College with more students on the first day than we had in Thailand after ten years? How do we feel about that? We are so proud that we send our best people and finances, and everything we can manage, to help him double as fast as possible. We believe in the people we love.

Faithfulness Filter

I once had a friend, or rather I thought he was a friend, who wanted to join with us in ministry in Thailand. We had opened the door to him and began to invest in the process. Then he met a missionary who had a flashier ministry down the road from us and began a courtship there. When I heard about his two-timing I realized our relationship did not have the potential of a marriage because he would apparently abandon me anytime someone prettier came along, and there's always someone prettier. I know guys who will only join something after it already looks good in the public eye, but they are afraid to invest when they are most needed, in the crucial time of start up. The rich guy isn't the one who bought his shares high; he's the one who invested in the launch. The people who gave to help Terry and I launch the ministry in Thailand are the most amazing people. They believed in us when we had nothing to show, and we hold them in the highest esteem.

What if one of our brothers has lost momentum? Should we look for someone else to hook up with? Absurd! One of the big advantages of covenant is that it carries us through the difficult times. It rallies and refocuses resources and support where most needed. The strong will share with the weak in their present need. We'll focus attention there and get that part of the ministry pruned up and growing again. I've had leaders do that for me on several occasions and I am so thankful for it. In fact, this ministry is still here because covenant brothers have carried us through times of trouble and weakness.

Many of our amazing guys who lead national ministries are guys who others had given up on. Pastor Ezekiel in Malaysia had given up on himself. He had a bad heart and he contacted me because he was looking for someone to take his church if he died. I flew down to Kuala Lumpur to meet and encourage him, we helped him with some of his medical costs. Ten years later he is doing wonderfully and leading several exciting churches. He was recently in India teaching in our Bible College there. We are so proud of him.

Investment Filter

As a leader of a band of covenant brothers, the best investment I can make is to invest in them.

Our ministry fiscal year begins each September when we kick off a new season by gathering our leaders from all our countries for a few days of apostolic and prophetic vision. It's not a conference where we have special speakers; it's just us, spending time together in prayer and fellowship to receive new direction and empowerment. These meetings are highly effective because we hear from everybody, and everybody gets refreshed, re-fired and ready to take on the world again. We always emerge from these times with a powerfully clear direction and affirmation of camaraderie. I love these leaders and I want them all to succeed exceptionally. Someone might say, "Yeah, because it makes you look good too. It's a win-win." Nope, that idea doesn't qualify because first of all, every victory is at the feet of Jesus and secondly, what happens across the nations is so out of my control that I would be a fool to take credit for it. I wake up every day amazed that God has given me a place to serve in this great vision.

Speech Filter

The way we talk about ourselves reveals who we love. As leaders you'll use your stories and experiences to teach others and that can naturally become a habit of talking about yourself. If you don't purposefully listen to others you'll soon become that guy who loves to hear himself talk.

I've got a good friend who likes to ask me questions specific to leadership challenges he is facing, but he never shuts up long enough for me to squeeze an answer in. Usually I have a one sentence answer, the one he needs because our ministry has already been through the things he is facing. I suppose I could get through to him with a text message or an email while he's talking, but he's not really listening anyway. If you don't listen you'll have to figure everything out for yourself.

On the other hand, sometimes it can be difficult to get the guys we lead to open up and talk. They want to but they need to feel confident that you are listening with an ear of love and not criticism or condemnation. We've all talked to leaders who will use our honest question as an opportunity to straighten us out... and then we get gun shy.

The first time Terry and I returned to Canada for a furlough we left the ministry in the charge of a young Canadian who even before we left began to refer to our staff as "my workers" and the ministry budget as "my finances." We returned a few months later to a royal mess of offended staff and empty bank accounts. The first indication of lacking or failed love comes in words; as we think in our hearts, so we speak.[c]

Nice Filter

Let me just mention once more, love does not behave rudely.

Have you ever given your wife the 'cold shoulder'? I have, hoping that this legalized form of torture will help her become the person I need her to be. It doesn't. Covenant ought to empower us to be nice to each other. A nice chat over a nice cup of tea is so much better.

To be nice, act nice: just smile, acknowledge people, take an interest in them and listen to them.

In our team we have developed a culture of being nice to each other. I've noticed that when people are nice to me I am willing to do about anything for them... and I am happy.

This Isn't About Me

Paul said, "If I have not love, I am nothing," and, "If I have not love, it profits me nothing."[d] In colloquial English, "If you don't love others you're a loser."

The converse would be equally true. Everything I am and everything I have comes out of this love, and the converse of nothing is everything! So I have a pretty amazing life, walking in covenant love. Jesus said, "If you cling to your life, you will lose it; but if you give up your life for me, you will find it."[e]

Give and it will be given back to you. You won't be left wanting.

(endnotes)

a Numbers 30:5 But if her father overrules her on the day that he hears, then none of her vows nor her agreements by which she has bound herself shall stand; and the LORD will release her, because her father overruled her.

b I Corinthians 13:4-8

c Matthew 12:34

d I Corinthians 13

e Matthew 10:39 NLT

Chapter 22

SHARED VISION

Get it right and it will grow.

Al Purvis

Back in the early '80's when I first wrote down our dreams for Asia, I had never heard anyone talk about vision. It was like nobody knew it was in the Bible. In fact, I showed an American friend my plans and he responded, "You're quite a visionary." That was the first time I heard the term in a Christian context, and I actually thought he was being sarcastic. Not long after we would hear endless sermons on Habakkuk chapter 2, "Write the vision and make it plain so that he that reads it can run with it."[a]

Habakkuk states the vision as, "Watch out for the proud, his heart is not upright in him, but the just will live by his faith."[b] The apostle Paul loved this vision and quoted it often in his New Testament teachings.

Habakkuk gave us two sides, the proud and the faithful; they apparently co-exist in the world of vision. He is exhorting us to know the difference and watch out for the proud ones. Two can't walk together unless they agree, so how do we know if we agree? We can agree if we can all see the same vision clearly... and in order to agree in a vision, it must be God's vision.

God's Vision

I don't follow another man's vision and I don't have a vision of my own. Habakkuk wasn't offering us a blank slate on which to write our own vision, that stuff has no end of troubles. But God already has a vision since before the world was formed that Jesus would be heir of the world and we would be His joint heirs. We are expected to take dominion and execute justice by declaring the Word of God and putting feet to those words.

When we agree on a vision, we're agreeing on God's vision. As a group with a common purpose, we're agreeing on a specific part of God's vision. That means that not just anybody can hook up with anybody, but that God's specific call on our lives will mesh into a certain part of His vision. There are people who are called to translate Bibles. We don't do that in our ministry, nor do we hold mass evangelism crusades. We plant churches and train disciples and we do a lot of other creative things as well in our efforts to plant churches and train disciples. But we don't all do the same things; we're called and equipped differently. Every member of the greater body supplies the part it's been given, and every gift has a place. We just need to know the ones we are to work in covenant with. They will be with us in the same vision and we can run together.

We have a vision statement. The wording changes a bit now and again, keeping current with culture and strategies. But it's really just a more personal and time-specific way to restate the Great Commission of Christ. The original one was in Greek anyway so we need a translation that clarifies our part and motivates us.

In our vision statement we stress the 'go' and the 'make disciples.' The greater body of Christ is to go into all the world, but our group is focused on Asia. I would love to go to Iran and Comoros and Brazil, and I would love to reach every strata of society, but we're just not big enough. We know where we are going and what we'll do when we get there, and it's something unique to us.

When Terry and I first arrived in Thailand we began to gather orphans. There was an estimated 100,000 who needed a home at that time. We could barley scratch the surface so we taught our 31 to become leaders. Six of them have founded businesses or ministries that teach children in our province alone. Last night Terry and I attended the graduation ceremony of an English nursery school operated by one of our adopted kids. Seventy influential people attended the gospel focused program where our kids presented the love of Jesus to them. This way the vision multiplies and it won't be long before 100,000 people will have had life changing experiences, because we landed here 30 years ago and did what we could.

Narrow Vision

The disciples we make turn out with the same characteristics as their teachers. They have the same values, passion, and purpose, and in those things we have a very specific, limited vision. Our vision does not call us to feed the poor in Comoros. The list of things we don't do is much longer than the list of things we do, and we hope that others are picking up and playing their part in the things we cannot do.

Empowering Others

A big leadership responsibility is to protect the time, energy, and resources of our team by disallowing expansion into the wrong good things. Re-envisioning helps to keep that focus clear and sharp. We have carved out a weekly time when I speak to our immediate Thailand team and we record these messages for our leaders around the world. I blog leadership principles for them and share other tools that might be helpful. We are in constant direct communication through social media and emails.

I just finished a series on the 'Ten Tenets of Victory,' adopted for Victory Asia and I added an eleventh that defines our particular ministry culture. Most of our national leaders are really good at passing the vision on down to their teams. Reminding people of who we are and what we are doing together keeps us on track as a ministry. We won't walk in covenant successfully if we don't spend time together.

We Believe

We are all looking for security on our investment. We're not going to work together with people who change directions and go the wrong way. There are some things that must never change. Along with the obvious unchangeables in our statement of faith, we must never waver from our foundational purposes either.

Don't we change with the times, with new understanding? The ministry is in a constant state of flux and change, and we love that part, but we must remember why we do what we do. The reason we began is the reason we must end with; that was our original intention, remember? We began with some very basic convictions. "We will walk in love and mercy" must never change for me.

Our conviction for success across Asia is built on these two unchangeable foundations: we work together through covenant relationships, not control, and we have a God-given purpose that we all agree on.

Anyone who deviates from these will go on without me.

(endnotes)

a Habakuk 2:2

b Habakuk 2:4

Chapter 23

COVENANT BOUND

Making our way powerful.

Al Purvis

A covenant of brothers puts the Lord in between us. Jonathan reminded David, "The Lord be between you and me forever."[a] With the Lord in between, God is the glue that holds us together. That's good, but now imagine the absolute assurance behind the promises we make to each other and the conviction behind the declarations of our faith, those things we intend to accomplish.

A covenant between men is only as secure as the ability of both men to keep it. But a covenant between brothers is secured by God - God gets in the middle. Same with marriage, the three-fold chord with God himself as one of the strands is not easily broken. Men are still fallible, but with God in the middle there is an anointing that connects the benefits of the covenant to each other with power.

With God in between, the promises and prophecies shared in covenant relationships are much more powerful than those from without. Jonathan declared David would become king, and he did. Their covenant played the key role in bringing God's plan to pass.

The other day Rich and I arrived at his home in the evening to find an amazing banquet set up in the yard to honour those who had worked so hard organizing the annual conference we had just finished. When they asked Rich to pray for the food he stood up and declared a new level of prosperity that would come on these leaders because they had invested such excellence in serving others. This was the word of the Lord and I just took a hold of it for all our ministries and leaders across Asia. I can have that word too because we are in covenant. What Rich's leaders get, we can all have and vice versa because God is in between. This is a powerful benefit of covenant.

I've noticed that leaders who love us will make the effort to speak into our lives, and often deliver prophetic words that become key turning points in our direction. I can't count how many times Rich has brought the word of the Lord to us, at the right season, words that we've used to set direction and build the ministry on. A couple months ago he came to Thailand with the prophetic word for our fourth decade of ministry. He prophesied that in the first ten years we had killed our lion, the next ten was the bear, the third decade brought Goliath down and now this would be our "Decade of Dominion." Imagine, I was standing on the threshold of decade number four, with something amazing stirring in my spirit, but I couldn't put words to it. Here comes a covenant brother to release the prophetic word for the next ten years. I am careful not to underestimate what that one word will produce all across Asia and beyond. There are some surprises in store for us.

I was in a mid-week service in Manila, preaching a word that God had given me earlier in the day and I watched it minister to Rich powerfully. He later said that it was the most powerful service he had been in for a long time, and we had just been in an absolutely amazing conference a week earlier. But what he meant was that this was more than just enjoyable and refreshing; something changed, something new was established and new direction was set. That's some of the fruit of a covenant relationship.

I love gathering with my covenant brothers and partners because something amazing always happens. God comes through and commands a special blessing.

The same thing happens when we pray together. We get special breakthroughs, big things happen and great results are obtained.

Prophetic Authority

Have you seen people lining up to receive the benefits of a covenant relationship without an equal commitment? I've seen prayer lines where everybody gets a 'double portion' of the anointing. But you don't get a double portion unless you are in covenant with the person who is giving the double portion, like Elisha's relationship with Elijah. That double portion cost Elisha his living and his life.

Authority to deliver God's gifts or prophetic words of direction to others comes in two ways; I'm talking about the serious stuff. The first criteria are accomplishments.

Accomplishments are credible evidence of God's blessing on your ministry. There are people who I've never met that I would love to receive a prophetic word from, or some other kind of empowerment from God, because they have a reputation of greatness in something that I also aspire to do. Some of the greatest prayers and prophetic words that Terry and I have received over the years have come from well-known ministers, people you only get to meet once and it's amazing. Those are like God-ordained coincidences, when God wants to get something to you that you don't have in your own circle of relationships.

The second thing is a level of relationship you have with some people. The other greatest prophetic words and impartations come from within our circle of relationships through people who know us inside and out and still love us. It's unlikely that anything significant will come through someone who has no reputation and is not connected through proven relationship. Usually they are flakes.

Impartation

Paul said, "I long to be with you that I may impart some spiritual gift to you that you may be established...."[b] He couldn't do that through a handkerchief or a prayer over the TV. Paul wrote the book of Romans as an apostle to the church in Rome, even though he had never been there. Many of them were converts of his ministry and trained by him to be leaders. They had been scattered from many places and gathered in Rome, and they planted this church. Paul obviously had no part or relationship with the property, building and the launch of the church or any of those things; his apostleship was only in relation to the people. He could speak to them with authority from a distance, and they received it because of who he was. But then he wanted to be there so he could impart a new level of what God wanted to establish in their lives.

These two things put God between us: our accomplishments and our level of relationship.

Authority is not about what men think you've accomplished;

it's about how you know God as He has moved through you to accomplish some things. There are people whose accomplishments are mainly in their prayer closet, and they carry the authority that comes with accomplishment. People who lack solid experience with God will simply lack authority when they speak.

My accomplishments are not a display of how amazing I am. The reason I'm the leader here is because I got here first and I've accomplished more than the others just because I've had more time to do it. It's not just opening your mouth and letting God fill it; it's how long and hard you have been fighting for your calling that establishes his ability and credibility in you.

Relationships

Relationships cost commitment. That commitment is the other currency that allows you to speak into the lives of other people. Some of my friends may seem a little loopy and you wonder why I listen to them. Well, it's because even though they've delivered some messages that fell off the table, they've also declared some other things that were right on. God uses them because they love me and so I listen to them.

Room for God in between us makes room for amazing things to happen.

(endnotes)

a I Samuel 20:23

b Romans 1:11

Chapter 24

COVENANT INTO THE NEXT

Succeeding to the next generations.

Al Purvis

I caught wind of a secret meeting that had taken place between a certain few of our Victory Asia Bible College students. The college year was coming to a close and they would soon leave each other and return to their respective countries. These are countries separated by thousands of kilometers, expensive air tickets, and the livelihood challenges of young men who were returning to some very poverty stricken areas of the world. Their concern wasn't just that they might never see each other again, but that they wanted each to do something for the other that would insure their dreams came true. They formed a covenant: each one would travel to the country of another at least once every two years to help him in the ministry. There were seven young men in all.

They had been watching Rich and I and the other apostolic leaders across Asia making great sacrifices to help each other and how those sacrifices had empowered successful ministry in each country. The young men followed suit. They have been traveling and helping each other. Joseph from India was one of those young men. Low caste and poor, the family sold whatever they had to get him to Thailand. It was enough to pay for his first term of Bible College. The rest of his tuition would have to come by greater faith.

Joseph finished two years and returned to India to launch a Bible College after the Thailand model. He opened with 25 students from all over India. Joseph has since traveled to Nepal to help Prem and Lalita, to Malaysia, the Philippines and Thailand to preach in our churches. He travels India by train, sometimes 45 hours non-stop, to gather potential leaders. He calls them "ordinary Indians becoming extraordinary leaders!"

I recently landed in Chennai. Joseph met me at the airport and we hurried to the train station. He said a short overnight ride would take us to his hometown and the new Bible College. The station was crammed, they all are, and Joseph pulled me along pointing out, "That train just came from Delhi, and that one is going to Kolkata." He loves to tell how these trains have taken him to every state in India in search of the right students for his Team Leadership College International. Even the name of his ministry stands in contrast to the insignificance of his town and his neighbourhood.

Joseph dreams big and he has a bent for illustration; "I'm like a train that carries anointing and vision from Thailand to India. The ministry base in Thailand is like a platform for us. See all these trains? They are nothing without this platform."

Without this apostolic connection and a covenant level of commitment to it, all of the ministries and projects we do would be like trains with nowhere to connect. They would be a big waste of resources. It's not that we're concerned about ministries wasting their money; this Kingdom is not built by money. But the disempowerment of covenant-less relationships is a waste of good lives and destinies.

In real terms this means that young men like Joseph, looking for somewhere to connect for the sake of a vision for his nation, googled something like "people in Asia with a vision for Asia" and our web page on Pakistan appeared first. There was a description and photos of the covenant relationship between our Thailand platform and our brothers in Pakistan. Joseph's heart was captured. He then had to resist the advice of the wise and even turn down an offer of money if he would 'abandon this silly dream.' Old school Christian leaders in India couldn't see how a ministry in Thailand would become a useful money connection for the future of a man like Joseph.

To the pure in heart, covenant speaks much more powerfully than money. Joseph studied for two years with a ministry family who are committed to visit India every year and help him. Actually teams from here, the Philippines and Malaysia have made a dozen trips there in the past two years and our Thailand team traveled the length of the country with him and his students. This comes as a great sacrifice to our missionaries who must pay for our own to travel to these ten nations. But carrying inspiration and equipping to new national leaders is worth any cost. These father-son covenant commitments are proving to be more powerful than anything else we could do.

The covenant relationships between our sons speak of a fruitful future. Long after us old guys are gone the young men and women will be running across Asia, bound together by covenant to sacrifice for the good success of each other.

Job said that not every grey head is wise, and we are

admonished to not follow just anybody, but follow those who through faith and patience inherit the promises.[a] I love being around people who have accomplished great things by faith and patience. I follow them because I want to do what they do.

So who's following me and you? Those of the next generation who aspire to do what we are doing. I was just in Pakistan helping Pastor Peter train his leaders. The young son of one of the pastors sat on the front row during every session. The ushers tried to send him away with the other kids to make room for more adults but he wouldn't go. After each session he came and complimented me on my message. His dream is to attend our Bible College in Thailand as soon as he is old enough. He watches every move I make and hangs on every word I speak. How great a responsibility do I carry for this young man's life? Be mindful, you are a hero to the next generation. What is it that they love about you?

For me, I love being around confidence, I love being around honour. I love watching an elderly man who walks like an ambassador, I love seeing 50-year-old couples holding hands, I love listening to kids talk to their parents.

We all aspire.

(endnotes)

a Hebrews 6:12

Chapter 25

LAST WORDS

Knowing what our future looks like.

Rich Conte

God calls people together in covenant relationships for a purpose. I believe there's always a purpose behind it. It's not just that, "I can be a blessing to you, you can be a blessing to me." If it's God then He has something bigger in mind. He's calling a group of people together into covenant relationship to accomplish something far larger than they could possibly accomplish alone.

Presently my team and I are based in the Philippines and Al and his team are based in Thailand. The Philippines has a very distinct call to send missionaries into all of Asia. It has been prophesied multiple times, more than I can count, that the Philippines will send out missionaries. Heidi Baker was in the Philippines recently and prophesied it again. She said that in five years the Philippines will have the most missionaries sent out into the world of any nation. She just felt that is the call of God on our nation.

Spiritually, Thailand is not nearly as Christian as the Philippines is, but geographically it is pretty much the most strategic place on the planet for reaching Asia. From Thailand you can go by land to Burma, Laos, Vietnam, Cambodia, Malaysia and China. There are several countries that you can drive to from Thailand. And now with the new ASEAN union opening up, English has been chosen as the official Asian language and all Asians can travel freely between these countries. Filipinos are the best English speakers and the most versatile travelers in all of Asia, by far. Besides being strategically located, Thailand is about the only country in Asia that has complete freedom of religion. And we feel called to send missionaries to Thailand.

God has positioned us and equipped us to play a key role in taking the Kingdom of God across Asia. What I see in our particular situation is that God has connected Pastor Al and me together to reach Asia for Christ. So God has built that covenant kind of relationship between the two of us. Not just to be a blessing to Al, not just to be a blessing to me, but because God has a far greater purpose, a far bigger plan than either one of us could accomplish on our own. So by bringing people together in covenant relationships, amazing things can happen. And all of us across Asia, we just love to be involved in the amazing things God is doing.

I see that in my lifetime, by the grace of God, we will plant hundreds of churches all throughout Asia as a direct result of covenant relationship. Could I have done that on my own? Not hundreds of churches. Maybe dozens. Maybe. Even that's a stretch. Could Pastor Al have done that by himself? He's probably better equipped than I am, but I don't know if he has the people. We've got the people; he's got the connections, the base, the strategies. So maybe I could have sent a dozen, two dozen missionaries, but together I honestly believe that we will see literally hundreds of churches planted throughout Asia. So covenant relationships are God-ordained for a bigger plan than any one or two people can fulfill on their own.

Finally, please take what you can from our story, and believe that God has more for you, something amazing. Don't hesitate to come into covenant with like-minded people, kindred spirits for the Great Commission, and go with God to the ends of the earth.

COVENANT OF BROTHERS

Connect with Rich Conte at: victoryasia.org

Connect with Al Purvis at: alpurvis.com

A big thanks to our Continuum Media team and friends for their diligent work in getting this book to print.

Tiffany Grant
Rebecca Watson
Carol Loewen
Dean & Sue Hughes
Kenn & Donna Haase
Kris Pagan
Penny Takahashi
Sawang & Lee-Anne Treetippayapitak
Terry Purvis